THE FATHERS
OF THE CHURCH

A NEW TRANSLATION

VOLUME 77

THE FATHERS
OF THE CHURCH

A NEW TRANSLATION

ST. CYRIL
OF ALEXANDRIA
LETTERS 51–110

Translated by

JOHN I. McENERNEY
Villanova University
Villanova, Pennsylvania

THE CATHOLIC UNIVERSITY OF AMERICA PRESS
Washington, D.C.

Nihil obstat:
REVEREND MICHAEL SLUSSER
Censor Deputatus

Imprimatur:
REV. MSGR. RAYMOND BOLAND
Vicar General for the Archdiocese of Washington

February 26, 1985

LIBRARY OF CONGRESS CATALOGING-IN-PUBLICATION DATA
(Revised for volume 2)

Cyril, Saint, Patriarch of Alexandria, ca. 370–444.
   St. Cyril of Alexandria.

   (The Fathers of the Church; v. 76-   )
   Includes bibliographies and indices.
   Contents: [1] 1–50 — [2] 51–110.
   1. Cyril, Saint, Patriarch of Alexandria, ca. 370–444.
   2. Christian saints—Egypt—Alexandria—Correspondence.
   I. McEnerney, John I., 1913-   . II. Title.
   III. Title: Saint Cyril of Alexandria.   IV. Series:
Fathers of the Church; v. 76, etc.
   BR60.F3C947   1987   270.21′092′4 [B]   85-5692
   ISBN 0-8132-0077-6 (v. 2)

CONTENTS

ABBREVIATIONS

LXX   *The Old Testament in Greek According to the Septuagint.* Ed. H. B. Swete. 3 volumes. Cambridge, 1887–94.

ODCC²   *The Oxford Dictionary of the Christian Church.* 2d and revised ed. Ed. F. L. Cross and E. A. Livingstone. Oxford, 1983.

PGL   *A Patristic Greek Lexicon.* Ed. G. W. H. Lampe. Oxford, 1961–1968.

Quasten   Johannes Quasten. *Patrology 3: The Golden Age of Greek Patristic Literature from the Council of Nicaea to the Council of Chalcedon.* Utrecht, 1960. Reprint Westminster, Md., 1983.

Schwartz, *Codex vaticanus gr. 1431*   E. Schwartz. *Codex vaticanus gr. 1431: Eine antichalkedonische Sammlung aus der Zeit Kaiser Zenos* in *Abhandlungen der Bayerischen Akademie der Wissenschaften philosophisch-philologische und historische Klasse.* Vol. 32. Abhandlung no. 6. Munich, 1927.

SELECT BIBLIOGRAPHY

TEXTS OF THE LETTERS

Bickell, Gustav. *Ausgewählte Schriften der Syrischen Kirchenväter Aphraates, Rabulas und Isaak von Ninive.* Kempten: Kösel, 1874.

Bouriant, U. *Fragments coptes relatifs au concile d'Éphèse.* Mémoires publiés par les membres de la mission archéologique française au Caire. Vol. 8. Paris, 1892.

Ebied, R. Y. and L. R. Wickham. *A Collection of Unpublished Syriac Letters of Cyril of Alexandria.* CSCO 360. Louvain, 1975.

————. "An Unknown Letter of Cyril of Alexandria in Syriac." *The Journal of Theological Studies* n.s. 22(1971): 420–434.

Evetts, B. *History of the Patriarchs of the Coptic Church of Alexandria.* Arabic text edited, translated and annotated. PO 1. Paris: Firmin-Didot, 1907. Pp. 433–436.

Guidi, I. *Atti della R. Accademia dei Lincei.* Ser. 4, rendiconti 2. Roma, 1886. Pp. 545–547.

Joannou, Périclès-Pierre. *Fonti: Fascicolo IX: Discipline générale antique (IVᵉ–IXᵉ s.).* Vol. 1, pt 2: *Les canons des Synodes Particuliers.* Vol. 2: *Les canons des Pères Grecs.* Pontificia commissione per la redazione del codice di diretto canonico orientale. Grottaferrata (Rome): Tipografia Italo-Orientale "S. Nilo," 1962–63.

Kraatz, Wilhelm. *Koptische Akten zum ephesinischen Konzil vom Jahre 431.* TU 11.2 n.s. Leipzig: Hinrichs, 1904.

Krusch, Bruno. *Studien zur christlich-mittelalterlichen Chronologie. Der 84 Jährige Ostercyclus und seine Quellen.* Leipzig: Von Veit, 1880.

Lebon, Joseph. *Scriptores Syri 46. Severi Antiocheni Liber contra impium Grammaticum. Orationis tertiae pars prior.* CSCO 94. Louvain: Durbecq, 1952.

Leipoldt, J. *Scriptores Coptici.* Series 2, volume 4: *Sinuthii archimandritae vita et opera omnia.* CSCO 42. Paris: Poussielgue, 1908.

Migne, J. P. ed. *S.P.N. Cyrilli Alexandriae Archiepiscopi Opera.* PG 76 and 77. Paris, 1863, 1859.

Overbeck, J. J. S. *Ephraemi Syri, Rabbulae Edesseni, Balaei Aliorumque opera selecta.* Oxford: At the Clarendon Press, 1865.

Pusey, P. E. *Sancti Patris Nostri Cyrilli Archiepiscopi Alexandrini in D. Joannis Evangelium. Accedunt fragmenta varia necnon tractatus ad Tiberium Diaconum duo.* Oxford: At the Clarendon Press, 1872.

xi

Richard, M. "Deux lettres perdues de Cyrille d'Alexandrie." *Studia Patristica* 7.1 (=TU 92). Éd. F. L. Cross. Berlin: Akademie Verlag, 1966. Pp. 274–275.

Schwartz, Eduard and Straub, John, et al. *Acta Conciliorum Oecumenicorum.* Berlin and Leipzig: de Gruyter, 1914–.

Schwartz, Eduard. *Codex vaticanus gr. 1431. Eine antichalkedonische Sammlung aus der Zeit Kaiser Zenos. Abhandlungen der Bayerischen Akademie der Wissenschaften philosophisch-philologische und historische Klasse.* Vol. 32. Abhandlung no. 6. Munich, 1927.

OTHER WORKS

Brown, Raymond E., Fitzmyer, Joseph, and Murphy, Roland E., eds. *The Jerome Biblical Commentary.* Englewood Cliffs, New Jersey: Prentice Hall, 1968.

Cross, F. L. and Livingstone, E. A., eds. *Oxford Dictionary of the Christian Church.* 2d and revised ed. Oxford: At the Clarendon Press, 1983.

Dombart, Bernard and Kalb, Alphonsus, eds. *S. Aurelii, De Civitate Dei Libri XI–XXII.* CCL 48. Turnhout: Brepols, 1955.

Du Manoir, Hubert, S. J. *Dogme et spiritualité chez saint Cyrille d'Alexandrie.* Paris: J. Vrin, 1944.

Festugière, A. J. *Éphèse et Chalcédoine Actes des Conciles.* Paris, 1982.

Garnier, Julian, ed., *Basilii Caesareae Cappadociae archiepiscopi opera omnia quae extant.* Paris: Gaume, 1839.

Geerard, Maurice. *Clavus Patrum Graecorum.* 4 vols. Turnhout: Brepols, 1974–1983.

Grillmeier, Aloys, S. J. *Christ in Christian Tradition.* Vol. 1: *From the Apostolic Age to Chalcedon (451).* 2d ed. Translated by John Bowden. Atlanta: John Knox Press, 1975.

Hefele, Charles, J. *A History of the Councils of the Church.* Edinburgh: Clark, 1883.

Hughes, Philip. *The Church in Crisis. A History of the General Councils 325–1870.* Garden City, N.Y.: Hanover House, 1961.

Jones, Charles, W. *Bedae Opera de Temporibus.* Cambridge, Mass.: The Medieval Academy of America, 1943.

Kelly, J. N. D. *Early Christian Doctrines.* 5th ed. London: Adam & Charles Black, 1977.

Lampe, G. W. H. *A Patristic Greek Lexicon.* Oxford: At the Clarendon Press, 1961–1968.

Liébaert, Jacques. *La doctrine christologique de saint Cyrille d'Alexandrie avant la querelle Nestorienne.* Lille: Economat, 1951.

Lindsay, W. M., ed. *Isidori Hispalensis Etymologiae.* Oxford: At the Clarendon Press, 1911.

Loofs, Friedrich Arnim. *Nestoriana: Die Fragmente des Nestorius gesammelt, untersucht und herausgegeben.* Halle: Niemeyer, 1905.

Morris, Rudolph, et al., trans. . . . *Vincent of Lerins: Commonitories* etc. FOTC 7. Washington, D.C.: The Catholic University of America Press, 1949.

Newman, Cardinal John Henry. *Tracts.* London: Longmans, 1924.

Orchard, Bernard et al., eds. *A Catholic Commentary on Holy Scripture.* New York: Thomas Nelson & Sons, 1953.

Papadopoulos, Chrysostom. *Ho Hagios Kurillos Alexandreias.* Alexandria: Patriarchal Press, 1933.

Quasten, Johannes. *Patrology.* 3 vols. Reprint Westminster, Md.: Christian Classics, 1983.

Schwartz, Eduard. *Christliche und Jüdische Ostertafeln. Abhandlungen der königlichen Gesellschaft der Wissenschaften zu Göttingen.* Philosophisch-Historische Klasse. Vol. 8.6 n.s. Berlin: Weidmann, 1905.

Smith, William and Wace, Henry. *A Dictionary of Christian Biography, Literature, Sects and Doctrines During the First Eight Centuries.* 4 vols. London, 1877–87.

Swete, Henry Barclay. *The Old Testament in Greek According to the Septuagint.* 3 vols. Cambridge: At the University Press, 1887–94.

Van den Dries, Joseph. *The Formula of St. Cyril of Alexandria.* Rome, 1937.

Way, Sister Agnes Clare, trans. *Saint Basil the Great: Letters Volume 2 (186–368).* FOTC 28. Washington, D.C.: The Catholic University of America Press, 1955.

Wickham, Lionel R. *Cyril of Alexandria. Select Letters.* Oxford: At the Clarendon Press, 1983.

Wiles, Maurice and Santer, Mark. *Documents in Early Christian Thought.* New York: Cambridge University Press, 1976.

Wilken, Robert L. *Judaism and the Early Christian Mind.* New Haven: Yale University Press, 1971.

Wolfson, H. A. *The Philosophy of the Church Fathers.* 3d ed. Cambridge, Mass.: Harvard University Press, 1970.

LETTERS

51–110

Letters 1–50 of Saint Cyril of Alexandria are in Volume 76 of The Fathers of the Church *series.*

LETTER 51

The letter of St. Sixtus, the Bishop [of Rome], to Cyril, the Bishop of Alexandria, after peace was made between Cyril and John.[1]

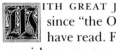ITH GREAT JOY WE[2] have been filled with eagerness since "the Orient from on high has visited us,"[3] as we have read. For behold, when we were anxious because we wish no one to perish, your holiness by your letters has indicated that the body of the church has been restored.[4] Since the structure in her members is being restored, we see that no one is wandering outside, because one faith testifies that all have been placed within. We rejoice that he[5] who caused this outrage has been removed from our midst.[6] He knows that what he thought has now been prejudicial to himself alone by his lack of faith, who fought against the one[7] who has been beneficial to all.

(2) But it is proper that we go from sadness over into joy, because he, in whose name the investigation has been proposed, since sorrow has now been lifted from the universal church, has furnished us with a period of rejoicing. Christ, our God, has shown how true is his cause[8] when he saw fit to

---

[1] For the critical text (only the Latin is extant) of this letter see Schwartz, *ACO* 1.2 pp. 107–108. Geerard numbers this letter 5351 in *CPG*.

[2] Sixtus III, Pope, A.D. 432–440.

[3] Cf. Lk 1.78. The quotation is appropriate since John of Antioch was the leader of the bishops of the East.

[4] A synod had assembled to celebrate the elevation of Sixtus to the Papacy and in a letter from him and the synod the labors of Cyril were approved and confirmed.

[5] Nestorius.   [6] Cf. 1 Cor 5.2.

[7] Here Cyril seems to be contrasted with Nestorius. Cyril was beneficial to all by resisting him; but this rather is understood to be Christ whose dignity Nestorius impugned.

[8] A different reading would give: "how truly the cause was his own."

3

arrange matters in such a way that he reserved the nature of so great a matter for the gathering of his bishops. The apostles when gathered together in one group often dealt with matters concerning the faith; and now the successors of the apostles, coming together in one group, give solemn thanks for the victory of the faith. O report[9] worthy of the one who sends it to us, worthy of the synod! Such a sign of joy in heaven deserved to have such inquirers. And since the matter and the case requires it, it is proper that the situation should not be hidden in silence.

(3) The entire brotherhood gathered together with the blessed apostle[10] Peter: What a fitting tribunal for the judges and suitable to the matters to be heard. Our fellow bishops had him[11] as a witness of their gratitude whom we have as the source of our honor. Over the holy and venerable synod which our birthday[12] had assembled with the Lord's blessing because such must be our faith, he himself presided, since it is proven that he was absent in neither spirit nor body. He was present for his palm of victory who did not fail in the contest. He came to the aid of our prayers who saw that the profession of faith which was handed down by him, the first of the apostles,[13] was being dishonored. He did not suffer a disgusting person[14] to rejoice in consolation nor did he long permit the purity of that spring to be disturbed by muddy water. Our brothers have returned to us, to us, I say, who by treating the disease with zeal for the common good have procured the health of their souls.

(4) John, our holy brother,[15] has not joined our exile;[16] he has not been deceived by the blasphemous preaching of that man for, as the outcome of affairs shows, he kept his opinion

[9] Cyril's report to Pope Sixtus.
[10] The reference is to Peter, as first Pope.
[11] Peter.
[12] Not the day of birth, but of his elevation to the Papacy. Schwartz comments that the date in question was July 31, A.D. 433.
[13] Cf. Mt 16.16.
[14] Nestorius. Sixtus does not name him in the letter at all.
[15] John of Antioch.
[16] John of Antioch did not condemn Nestorius at Ephesus.

suspended and did not deny it. For what else can be said in judgment of the inventor of evils except [17] what was approved for us to think by him whose cause was being pleaded by his own priests. Indeed John had decided concerning the deserter from our camp [18] that which his treachery induced the leaders of the faith to pass as judgment on him. John would never have separated himself from our number, to which he was also able to return.

(5) Rejoice, dearest brother, and since our brothers have been reconciled to us, rejoice as a victor. The church has been seeking for those whom she has received back. For if we wish none of the little ones to perish [19] how much more should we rejoice at the sanity of the just? We read about how much joy the return of a single sheep furnished,[20] and accordingly we should undertand how much praise the recalling of so many shepherds should have. The flocks are envisaged in the individual nor is the case of just one treated here, as often as there is question of the health of many.[21] We rejoice that we have done nothing premature here, when we are pleased at the fruit of our long suffering. We sustained our brothers, certain that they would bring forth not thorns but grapes. The harvest of our joys is in evidence which filled the holy synod with lavish thanksgiving. That guardian cares for his vineyard who the prophet David testifies neither slumbers nor sleeps in protecting the house of Israel.[22] Flame has seized upon that branch which is sterile to our Christ and does not bring forth fruit.[23] But just as we see that this is proper for the one condemned, so it is fitting to say about the brothers who have been returned to us that the planting which the Father has planted was not able to be uprooted by the devil.[24] Therefore eternal fire claimed that sterile branch for itself, but the vineyard of the eternal owner [25] has claimed these others so much so that

[17] Another reference to Nestorius. Christ's cause was defended at Ephesus against him.
[18] Nestorius.
[19] Cf. Mt 18.14.
[20] Cf. Lk 15.6 and Mt 18.13.
[21] Cf. Mt 7.16
[22] Cf. Ps 120(121).3–4.
[23] Cf. Jn 15.2, 6 and Mt 7.19.
[24] Cf. Mt 15.13.
[25] Cf. Mt 20.8, 9.

we rejoice that the priest of the Church of Antioch is now called by your holiness a venerable man and lord.[26] And rightly is he called a lord who has recognized our common Lord and confesses the mystery of his Incarnation in a voice catholic with us.

(6) Your fraternity[27] has narrated well and briefly for us what was done about this same matter; yet we have not been astonished to read the insult of the deposition against you composed by those who disagreed. For we have often realized that truth is made plain by calumnies nor is it ever able to be conquered by falsehood. The devotees of falsehood are always a vexation to one who is preaching the faith. For there is prepared "a great reward in heaven"[28] with happiness for those on whom it is enjoined to suffer reproaches, persecutions and all evil for the sake of justice. You have endured falsehood so that you might make truth the victor; and so now we should scoff at falsehood, since no man could perish for the truth.

(7) We are awaiting, therefore, the clerics of our brother John just mentioned and we desire them to come, and we know that they are responsive in consideration of your honor and toil. As we already have often written to our brother and fellow bishop Maximian, you yourself are not adverse to opening a door for those returning, so that truly "not one of them perished except the son of perdition"[29] and that there might be for him the greater reason for bewailing, because he alone deserved to be excluded.

(8) The holy brotherhood with me writes these words to your holiness approving in all things and confirming your labors which cannot, however, be heavy or bitter because they have been expended for him whose "light burden and easy yoke"[30] we bear.

(9) Given on the fifteenth of the Kalends of October, in the fourteenth consulship of Theodosius and Maximus.[31]

---

[26] In the salutation of the letter which Cyril wrote to John, Letter 39, he calls him lord.

[27] Cyril.

[28] Cf. Mt 5.11, 12.

[29] Cf. Jn 17.12.

[30] Cf. Mt 11.30.

[31] Schwartz dates this letter September 17, A.D. 433.

LETTER 52

Sixtus, to John, the Bishop of Antioch.[1]

F YOUR CHARITY would deign to consider the glory of the body of the church and its integrity, assuredly it would not need someone to explain our joy. For events themselves most plainly relate that our sorrow was suddenly changed into joy by the message of our holy brother Cyril. It delights us that we have escaped from this great anxiety since your holiness proved to be the acme of our faith for the culprit.

(2) Now truly he[2] knows that he is an exile,[3] now he knows that he has been cast out. There is an abundance of thorns[4] for him in the desert, for the grapes which he gathered are failing him. These are the fruits which he has who did not employ husbandry toward the vineyard of our Lord. I believe that that order of the course of events has come to your charity[5] as we desired to come to his aid by our admonition.[6] We held him back when he was going headlong who would have been submerged into the depths by the weight of his blasphemies. If we shall weigh impartially the nature of the business by a just scale, Nestorius will seem to no one to have been condemned too late. This would have been a due statement in the past.[7] Now we are enjoying the good things of the present

[1] For the critical text (only the Latin is extant) of this letter, a companion to the preceding, see Schwartz, *ACO* 1.2 pp. 108–110. Geerard numbers this letter 5352 in *CPG*.
[2] Nestorius.
[3] Nestorius was effectively exiled partly through John.
[4] Cf. Mt 7.16.
[5] John of Antioch.
[6] Popes Celestine and Sixtus wished to save Nestorius if he would recant.
[7] The condemnation came at the right time.

nor should we cling to our sorrows to whom the Lord has granted rejoicing.

(3) All the brethren have heard who have gathered for the anniversary of my election that you acknowledge me as presiding in the apostolic see for the welfare of the human race.[8] Although they exceed my merit and although I know that these would exist without me, I willingly accept the exordium of your message, because you must not suffer a contradiction, you who confess Christ our Lord for the good of the human race, just as he was born.

(4) Later you add that I am a light-bearer for the church and one who gives light for all. And we confess that you also are now light-bearers even as we are, who bear the sign of that light on our brow. Therefore, let all priests of the Lord who preach the faith be light-bearers and shed their light everywhere.

(5) And may Nestorius also be that light-bearer of whom it is written: "Lucifer fell, who rose in the morning."[9] He fell, but it was in his pride; he fell, but he was dashed headlong when he determined to ascend into heaven and to place his throne above the stars of the sky, and tried to assure the most high that he was like unto him. Lucifer boasts he will be like the most high; Nestorius tried to call down the most high unto his own likeness. For he preached that he was begotten only as a man, thus taking away the mystery of his Incarnation, and cancelling it, or, I should say, attacking that by which our faith and our salvation subsists according to the creed of our faith. But this is not the time of strife, since the enemy lies prostrate. We must pass on from these matters which brought on the strife. It is inopportune in a time of victory to discuss the battles still.

(6) What confidence in our actions can be more evident, what reckoning greater than the palm of victory?[10] With the help of the Lord let us enjoy a good and happy outcome be-

---

[8] Schwartz notes that this was July 31, A.D. 433.

[9] Cf. Is 14.12. Note the play on words involved in the reference.

[10] Understood in the thought is: won against the adversaries of the faith. The argument of Sixtus depends on 1 Jn 5.4.

cause again brethren are beginning to dwell together as one.[11]
We desire your holiness to preach what you write. You have
experienced by the outcome of the present matter what it is to
think with us. Blessed Peter handed on in his successors[12]
what he received. Who would wish to be separated from the
doctrine of the one who the master taught was first among the
apostles? He was not instructed by hearing him through someone else; a statement he read did not instruct him; he was
taught by the mouth of the teacher along with the other apostles. He did not endure an inquiry into what was written in
Scripture nor into who wrote it; he received an absolute and
simple faith and one which had no controversy, which we indeed ought always to meditate upon and remain in, so that, by
following the apostles in the true meaning of the word, we
may deserve to be among those who are apostolic. No small
burden, no small labor weighs upon us, namely, that the
Church of the Lord may be without stain.[13]

(7) The care of our most clement and most Christian rulers
testifies how much we ought always to be anxious about this.
Behold, most dear brother, how vigilantly they bend themselves to their heavenly task. They have known no holidays[14]
in their thoughts nor have they deigned to care for earthly
things unless they have complied with heavenly ones. How
often has their word aroused the faith of the apostles and
brothers who were divided? They bend themselves to his business who has never refused his aid to their power. They know
that he is interested in their care who will return it at great
interest. We must glory in this fact because we see that our
earthly kings have our celestial king allied with them. They
give heed, as David says, and those who judge the earth have
been instructed,[15] since, as he says elsewhere, they and all
people praise the name of the Lord.[16]

(8) Therefore, since as the apostle says, "the faith is one,"[17]

[11] Cf. Ps 132(133).1.   [12] The Apostolic See.
[13] Cf. Eph 5.27.   [14] That is, carefree days.
[15] Cf. Ps 2.10.   [16] Ps 148.14.
[17] Eph 4.5.

which also has prevailed victoriously,[18] let us believe what must be stated and let us state what we must maintain. Let nothing further be allowed for novelty because it is proper that nothing be added to our ancient tradition.[19] Let the lucid and clear faith of our ancestors be disturbed by no admixture of uncleanness. The faith has a man approved by us, our brother and fellow bishop Maximian, the priest of the Church of Constantinople, consecrated there by a divine judgment, so that the successful sweetness of his simplicity may overcome the sickness of the disease which one man's trickery had poured out as poisons,[20] nor will he who sides with us be able to preach anything there other than what we believed and what he has frequently heard from our predecessors.

(9) Given on the fifteenth of the Kalends of October in the fourteenth consulship of Theodosius and Maximus.[21]

[18] Cf. 1 Jn 5.4.
[19] Schwartz notes that this paragraph up to here has been quoted in the *Commonitories* of St. Vincent of Lérins. See FOTC 7.330.
[20] Nestorius's teachings as opposed to Maximian's.
[21] September 17, A.D. 433; cf. note 31 of the previous letter.

LETTER 53
(Fragments) [1]

Cyril, to Sixtus, [2] the Bishop of Rome.

 OR I NEVER am accused of having thought anything different from the truth in my opinions, nor have I ever said that the divine nature of the Word was subject to suffering.

[And, after other passages:]

(2) I know that the nature of God is impassible, unchangeable, and immutable, even though by the nature of his humanity Christ is one in both natures and from both natures.

---

[1] For the text of this fragment edited by Cardinal Mai see Migne, PG 77.285–288. Geerard numbers this letter 5353 in *CPG*.

[2] The text has been corrected from *Iouston* in the Greek.

11

LETTER 54

A letter of Cyril, to Eusebius, a priest.[1]

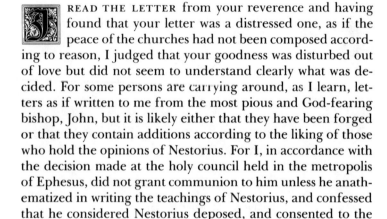 READ THE LETTER from your reverence and having found that your letter was a distressed one, as if the peace of the churches had not been composed according to reason, I judged that your goodness was disturbed out of love but did not seem to understand clearly what was decided. For some persons are carrying around, as I learn, letters as if written to me from the most pious and God-fearing bishop, John, but it is likely either that they have been forged or that they contain additions according to the liking of those who hold the opinions of Nestorius. For I, in accordance with the decision made at the holy council held in the metropolis of Ephesus, did not grant communion to him unless he anathematized in writing the teachings of Nestorius, and confessed that he considered Nestorius deposed, and consented to the consecration of the most pious and most God-fearing bishop, Maximian.

(2) But when the most God-fearing Bishop of Emesa, Paul, had suffered a thousand woes at the hands of those deposed, I mean, Helladius, Eutherius, Dorotheus, and Himerius,[2] and when he urged that the discussion in their regard would have a prototype in the peace of the churches, I said in answer that I am holding no discussion of those who have been deposed, but that it is necessary that they remain in the same position in which they are also banded together. But I pardoned them for the contumely inflicted on me by them.[3] It was not suitable

---

[1] For the critical text of this letter see Schwartz, *ACO* 1.1.7 pp. 164–165. Geerard numbers this letter 5354 in *CPG*.

[2] Cf. Letter 11, note 3, and Letters 48 and 90.

[3] John of Antioch and his bishops.

---

that the churches be split into divergent opinions for the sake of this reason only, since what is more necessary was being brought to completion, I mean, that those who long ago refused to do it should anathematize the teachings of Nestorius, and approve his deposition.

(3) And they confessed in writing that the Holy Virgin is the Mother of God and that the only begotten Son of the Father, who was begotten before all ages, in recent ages of time was begotten according to the flesh from a woman,[4] and that the person[5] of the Son is one, and that the theologians refer some of the apostolic and evangelical statements[6] to his divinity and others in turn to his humanity. For Nestorius, by dividing into two the one Son and Christ and Lord, set the man separate and apart from the Son, and the Word of God separate and apart from another son. And he said that some of the statements are those of the man, and others are those of the Word of God.

(4) But the orthodox doctrine concerning Christ does not have it so. We know that there is one Son and Christ and Lord who is God and man, and we state that the divinity is his and likewise also the humanity is his. For he sometimes speaks divinely as God and he sometimes speaks humanly as man. Therefore since they[7] confessed these doctrines, how was it anything but excessive of them to fight still against those who did not want the schism to prevail and incline the churches in the East into heresy? Would that all the other bishops were so disposed.

(5) For even though Helladius of Tarsus and some others did not have orthodox opinions, this was nothing against those who chose to hold orthodox doctrines. Let two or three depart, if they wish, so long as the churches everywhere hold one and the same faith. And let your reverence not be ignorant of the following. For when Paul, the Bishop of Emesa who was mentioned earlier, came to Alexandria, he said that some of those with your piety told lies to the effect that you

[4] Cf. Gal 4.4.   [5] πρόσωπον.
[6] i.e., those made by our Lord in the Gospels.
[7] John of Antioch and his bishops.

said that the nature of the divinity was capable of suffering, that the Word brought down his flesh from heaven, and that afterwards he endured change in the nature of the flesh. It was necessary, therefore, that the errors of these liars be made manifest to those who are rather simple, so that they may not be scandalized by their chattering.

(6) Because of this, when writing to the most God-fearing Bishop of Antioch, John, I derided their calumnies. For I did not arrive at this opinion out of a change of mind, nor do I find that I ever said such a thing in a volume or a letter or a book. Neither do we at all know what on earth the word co-essentiation[8] means. And it is likely that those who write such things there, when defending themselves for the vehemence which we endured at Ephesus, are inventing such words in order that they may not seem to have been disturbed in vain. For their consciences are accusing them. Therefore, let your reverence speak out against those who are saying some things there in place of others, for everything has safely come to pass.

(7) And the beloved Casius the deacon is one of those who departed and arrived in Antioch and is able to say how many days he spent there without giving to John the letter of communion unless he first wrote a letter with his own hand concerning all these matters.

[8] συνουσίωσις, "fusion of essences."

LETTER 55

A letter of the same on the holy creed. To the beloved and most desired Anastasius, Alexander, Martinian, John, Paregorius, the priest, Maximus the deacon, and the other orthodox fathers of monks, and to those living the solitary life with you secure in the faith of God, Cyril sends greetings in the Lord.[1]

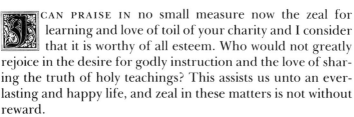CAN PRAISE IN no small measure now the zeal for learning and love of toil of your charity and I consider that it is worthy of all esteem. Who would not greatly rejoice in the desire for godly instruction and the love of sharing the truth of holy teachings? This assists us unto an everlasting and happy life, and zeal in these matters is not without reward.

(2) Our Lord Jesus Christ somewhere says to God his Father in heaven, "Now this is everlasting life, that they may know you, the only true God, and him whom you have sent, Jesus Christ."[2] Faith that is true and not subject to derision, because it has the brilliance attendant on good works, fills us with every good and reveals those who have found illustrious glory. The splendor of our actions if it appears to have no share in orthodox teachings and blameless faith would not at all benefit the soul of man, in my opinion. Just as "faith without works is dead,"[3] so also we say that the reverse is true. Therefore let integrity in faith shine forth along with the glories of upright living. Thus we shall be perfect according to the Law of the all-wise Moses, "You shall be perfect," he says, "before the Lord your God."[4]

---

[1] For the critical text of this letter see Schwartz, *ACO* 1.1.4 pp. 49–61. Geerard numbers this letter 5355 in *CPG*. See also Ebied-Wickham, *Unpublished Syriac Letters*, 1–19, and Wickham, *Select Letters*, 94–131.

[2] Jn 17.3.   [3] Cf. Jas 2.20.

[4] Dt 18.13.

(3) Those who out of ignorance have belittled possession of the true faith, and then exalt their way of life with virtuousness, somehow are like to men who have goodly features of face but the glance of their eyes is irregular and distorted. Proper to them is the saying of God through the voice of Jeremiah to the mother of the Jews, I mean Jerusalem, "Behold, your eyes are not true and your heart is not fair."[5] Accordingly it is necessary that, before other things, you have a sound mind within yourselves and that you be mindful of Holy Scripture addressing you and saying, "Let your eyes look straight ahead."[6] The right sight of the eyes hidden within is to be able to see plainly and subtly, insofar as is allowed, whatever considerations there may be concerning the words of God. "For we see through a mirror in an obscure manner and we know in part"[7] but "he who discloses the recesses of the darkness"[8] sends the light of truth to those who wish to gain a knowledge concerning him rightly. It is necessary therefore that we prostrate ourselves before God saying, "Give light to my eyes that I may not sleep in death,"[9] for to slip away from the rightness of holy doctrines would be nothing else except to sleep in death and we depart from this rightness when we do not follow the divinely inspired Scriptures.

(4) Either by unpraiseworthy preconceptions or by a partiality toward some who are not walking rightly with regard to the faith, we are overpowered because we share the inclinations of their minds and above all else do damage to their souls. Therefore we must believe those who are in charge of rightness in thinking about the holy Gospels which, through the Holy Spirit, "they who from the beginning were eyewitnesses and ministers of the word have handed down to us,"[10] whose footsteps our all-glorious Fathers were zealous to follow, who assembled at Nicaea in a period of crisis and defined the venerable and universal profession of the faith. Christ himself was seated in council with them for he says, "Where

5 Jer 22.17.
7 Cf. 1. Cor 13.12.
9 Ps 12 (13).4.

6 Prv 4.25.
8 Cf. Jb 12.22.
10 Lk 1.2.

two or three are gathered together in my name, there am I in the midst of them."[11]

(5) How is there doubt that Christ was invisibly presiding over that holy and great council? A certain groundwork and unbreakable and unshaken foundation for mankind throughout the world was thrown up, or rather put down, which is the sincere and blameless confession of faith. Then how was Christ not present if indeed he was the foundation according to the statement of the most wise Paul, who says, "For another foundation no one can lay but that which has been laid, which is Jesus Christ."[12]

(6) Therefore, the holy Fathers who were with them, shepherds of the people, luminaries of the churches, and most skillful teachers of the mysteries have protected unexceptionably the faith set forth and defined by them. In the confessions or expositions of the Fathers one would see nothing whatever omitted or overlooked of what is necessary for our benefit, for they fashioned them concerning the true and unadulterated faith for the refutation and ruin of all heresy and unholy loquacities, and for the strengthening and safety of those who walk rightly with regard to the faith. For them the light-bearing lamp has risen and "the day dawns" according to the Scriptures[13] and to them the light of truth is sent which is the grace of the Holy Spirit.

(7) Since your reverence has written that some are diverting what is in the creed into a channel which is not the proper one either because they do not understand the meaning of the words in it or because they are carried away to wrong thinking by an inclination toward the writings of certain men, I thought that it was necessary for me also to address my words to you on these very matters and clearly interpret the meaning of the exposition of faith and to state in summary the thoughts that come into my mind. We follow in every way the confessions and doctrines of the holy Fathers while we rightly and unswervingly prove what was said by them. Already the holy

[11] Mt 18.20.   [12] 1 Cor 3.11.
[13] Cf. 2 Pt 1.19.

council, which assembled in Ephesus according to the will of
God, when it brought in a holy and accurate decision against
the evil doctrine of Nestorius, condemned along with him, by
imposing a just sentence upon them, the "profane novelties" [14]
of others, who either might exist after him or even had
existed before him, because they had the same teachings as he
had and dared to speak or write about them. And it followed,
since one man was condemned once because of such "profane
novelties," that they should go against not one man but, so to
speak, against their whole heresy, that is, the calumny which
they have fashioned against the holy dogmas of the church by
preaching two sons, dividing the indivisible, and registering
against heaven and earth the accusation of adoring a man. [15]

(8) The holy multitude of spirits above adores with us the
one Lord Jesus Christ. So that some may not be ignorant
of the meaning of the creed which prevails and has been
preached in all the holy churches of God, I inserted the doctrines, that is, the expositions of the holy Fathers in the com-
mentaries made there, in order that those who read them may
know in what way it is proper to understand the exposition of
the holy Fathers which is the pure creed of the true faith. I
think that your charity also read the book which we have composed on these very matters. After I have set before you now,
as I said, the very symbol itself word for word, I shall turn myself with the help of God to the clear interpretation of each of
the matters which are in it, for I know that the all-glorious
Peter has written, "Be ready always with an answer to everyone who asks a reason for the hope that is in you." [16]

THE CREED OF THE FATHERS AT NICAEA

(9) We believe in one God, the Father almighty, creator of all
things visible and invisible, and in one Lord Jesus Christ, the
only begotten Son of God, begotten of the Father, that is,

[14] 1 Tim 6.20.   [15] ἀνθρωπολατρεία.
[16] 1 Pt 3.15.

from his substance, God of God, light of light, true God of true God, begotten not created, consubstantial with the Father, through whom all things were made both in heaven and on earth, who for us men and for our salvation descended, and was incarnate, and was made man, suffered, and rose again on the third day, ascended into heaven, and is coming to judge the living and the dead; and in the Holy Spirit.

(10) Those who say: "There was a time when he was not, and he was not before he was begotten, and that he was made from non-existence, maintaining that he is of another *hupostasis,* or another substance, or that the Son of God is mutable or subject to change," these the Catholic and Apostolic Church anathematizes.

(11) They said that they believe in one God because they were overthrowing as if from the very foundations the opinions of the pagans, "for professing themselves to be wise they became fools. And they changed the glory of the incorruptible God into the likeness of the image of a corruptible man and of birds and of four-footed beasts and of creeping things."[17] And they adored "the creature instead of the creator,"[18] and they have been slaves to the elements of the world thinking that there are many, even countless, gods. Therefore for the destruction of the error of polytheism they name one God following in every way the Holy Scriptures and showing the beauty of the truth to all men throughout the whole world under the sun. The all-wise Moses did this also saying most clearly, "Hear, O Israel! The Lord your God is one Lord."[19] And he says somewhere, the creator and Lord of all, "You shall not have other gods besides me."[20] And besides through the voice of the holy prophets, "I am first and I am after this; besides me there is no God."[21] Excellently, therefore, did the most glorious Fathers, when laying down as the foundation for the faith that it is necessary to think and say that God is one and alone by nature and in truth, say that they believe in one God.

[17] Rom 1.22, 23.   [18] Rom 1.25.
[19] Dt 6.4.   [20] Ex 20.3.
[21] Cf. Is 44.6.

(12) And they also call him Father almighty in order that there may be brought in with the Father the manifestation of the Son, through whom he is the Father, subsisting with him and always coexisting. For he was not the Father in time, but always was what he is, that is, the Father, being beyond everything which is made and in the highest heights. For to rule and be Lord of all gives to him such brilliant and incomparable glory.

(13) Moreover they state that by him has been made everything which is in heaven and upon earth, so that his supereminence in regard to all creation may thus be known. For the difference of creator and creature, of unbegotten and begotten, of a nature under the yoke and slavery and a nature bedecked with the dignities of the master and possessing divine and supramundane glory is inestimable.

(14) Yet when they spoke of the Son, in order that they may not seem to attribute an ordinary name to him, one which perhaps could be assigned even to us ourselves, for we are also called sons,[22] they very prudently affix those names by which it is possible to see the brilliance of the natural glory which is in him above creation. For they say that he was begotten not created, knowing him to be in essence untouched by creation by not being created, but rather affirming confidently that he was begotten of the essence of God the Father independently of time and incomprehensibly for "in the beginning was the Word."[23] Then when signifying exceedingly well the reality of the begetting, and let this be said in human fashion because of usage, they state that God the Son was begotten of God. For where there is in short a true begetting, it would by all means follow there that it is necessary to think and say that the begotten is not of another substance than the begetter, but is of the substance of his begetter, because he is of it according to any consideration fitting and congruent to it.

(15) The incorporeal will not beget according to the body, but rather in this way, namely, as light of light, so that the light which has shone forth would be known to be in the light

---

[22] Cf. Gal 4.6.   [23] Jn 1.1.

which flashed forth, to be from it according to an unspeaka-
ble and ineffable procession, and to be in it according to unity
and identity of nature. Thus we say the Son is in the Father,
and the Father in the Son. The Son typifies his own begetter
in his own nature and glory. He said clearly to one of his holy
disciples, and this was Philip, "Do you not believe that I am in
the Father and the Father in me? He who has seen me has
seen the Father."[24] "I and the Father are one."[25] Accordingly
he is consubstantial with the Father. Thus also it is believed
that true God was begotten of true God.

(16) And we will find the word begetting applied also to
creatures, I mean according to what was said by God concerning those of the blood of Israel, "Sons have I reared and
raised."[26] However, the creature enjoys such an appellation in
the order of love. But there is nothing by way of misapplica-
tion in the case of his Son by nature, but it is true in every way,
and because of this, alone of all he says, "I am the truth."[27] So
that if one should use the word begetting or sonship about
him, he would in no way be speaking falsehood, for he is the
truth. Accordingly the all-holy doctors are protecting our
souls by speaking everywhere of the Father and of the Son
and of begetting and saying true God of true God and that
light shone forth from light, so that the begetting might be
incorporeal and simple and have the concept of being from
him and in him and that each subsists in his own person, for
the Father is the Father and not the Son, and the Son is the
one begotten and not the Father; and in identity of nature
proper to each is to be what he is.

(17) But although they stated that the Father is creator of all
things visible and invisible, they say that all things were made
through the Son, not because they have assigned less glory as
a certain lot proper to him, far from it. For how at all events is
it possible to see more or less in identity of substance? But they
are saying that God the Father does not by nature make or call
into being anything in any other way than through the Son in

[24] Cf. Jn 14.8–10.   [25] Jn 10.30.
[26] Is 1.2.   [27] Jn 14.6.

the Spirit as through his own power and wisdom. For it is written that, "By the word of the Lord the heavens were made; and by the spirit of his mouth all their host."[28] And assuredly the all-wise John when he said, "In the beginning was the Word, and the Word was with God; and the Word was God"[29] necessarily added, "All things were made through him, and without him nothing was made."[30]

(18) Accordingly after they had pointed out that the Son is consubstantial, equal in honor, and equal in operation to the Father, they fittingly speak of his Incarnation and declare the mystery of the dispensation with flesh judging quite rightly that the tradition of the faith will be most perfect and because of this self-sufficient. It is not enough for those who believe in him just to be convinced and to think that God was begotten of God the Father being consubstantial with him and "the image of his substance."[31] It was necessary to know in addition to these that for the sake of the salvation and the life of all having lowered himself to an emptying he took "the form of a slave"[32] and came forth as man begotten according to the flesh from a woman.[33]

(19) Because of this they say, "who for us men and for our salvation descended, and was incarnate, and was made man." Behold, how the statement progresses for them in the proper order and in the most fitting arrangement. They say that he descended in order that by this we should know that the Lord is above all in nature and in glory, and again that he came down for our sake, I mean unto a desire to come to a likeness to us and in flesh to shine upon the world, for it is written in the book of Psalms, "God will visibly come, our God, and he will not be silent."[34]

(20) But his descent might be understood, if one should choose, in another fashion, that is, as a descent from heaven, or from above, or from his Father. It is usual in the Holy Scriptures to clarify what is above thought by words suited to

[28] Cf. Ps 32 (33).6.
[30] Jn 1.3.
[32] Phil 2.7.
[34] Ps 49 (50).3. (LXX)
[29] Jn 1.1.
[31] Heb 1.3.
[33] Cf. Gal 4.4.

us. And therefore he said when conversing with the holy disciples, "I came forth from the Father and have come into the world. Again I leave the world and go to the Father,"[35] and again, "You are from below, I am from above,"[36] and besides these, "I came forth from the Father and I have come."[37] The divinely inspired John writes, "he who comes from above is over all."[38] Although being in the highest heights and according to substance above all with his own Father seeing that he is crowned in identity of nature with him "he did not consider being equal to God a thing to be clung to, but emptied himself, taking the form of a slave and being made like unto men. And being found in form as a man he humbled himself."[39]

(21) For when the Word being God put on our flesh, even so he remained God and for this reason the most holy Paul says that he was made like unto men and appeared in the form of man. For he was God, as I said, in a form like unto us, and not having taken inanimate flesh, as it seems good to some of the heretics to think, but rather flesh animated with a rational soul. Therefore the Fathers said that he, the Word which came forth from the substance of the Father, the only begotten Son, true God of true God, light of light, through whom all things were made, descended, and was incarnate, and was made man, that is, endured birth according to the flesh from a woman, and came forth in our form, for this is being made man.

(22) Therefore there is one Lord Jesus Christ, the very only begotten Word of the Father made man, who did not relinquish being what he was, for he remained God in his humanity, master in the form of a slave, having in the emptying like unto us the fullness of divinity, being in the weakness of the flesh the Lord of power, and in the measure of his humanity having as his own that which is above all creation. For, what he was before the flesh, he has, being incapable of losing it, for he was God, true Son, the only begotten, light, life, and power. But what he was not, these he is seen to have taken in addition through the Incarnation, for he made his own what is of the

---

35 Jn 16.28.
37 Jn 16.28.
39 Phil 2.6, 7.

36 Jn 8.23.
38 Jn 3.31.

flesh. The flesh was not that of some one else, but rather his own ineffably and unspeakably united to him. And thus John wisely says, "The Word was made flesh."[40] And he became flesh not because he turned into the nature of the flesh according to a transition, or a change, or an alteration, nor because he underwent a confusion, or a blending, or the fusion of essences being babbled about by some, for that is impossible since he is by nature unchangeable and is unalterable, as I said, but because he took flesh animated with a rational soul from a virginal and undefiled body and made it his own.

(23) But it is at times a usual thing in the divinely inspired Scripture to signify the entire man by only the flesh, for it says, "For I will pour out a portion of my spirit upon all flesh."[41] God did not promise that he would send his Spirit to flesh not animated with a rational soul but rather to men who are composed of soul and body. Therefore, the Word became man without ceasing to be what he was, but he has remained the Word even when he appeared in a form like unto us.

(24) Nor is a man first known to be Christ and then so progresses unto being God, but the Word, being God, became man in order that in the same being it might be known that God himself was nevertheless also man. However those who divide him into two sons and dare to say that God the Word joined to himself the man of the seed of David and shared with him the glory, the honor, and the excellence of the filiation, and prepared him to endure the cross, to die, to rise again, to ascend into heaven, and to sit at the right hand of the Father, in order that he might be adored by all creation and receive the honors by a relationship to God, in the first place preach two sons and in the second place ignorantly distort the meaning of the mystery. For, as I said, Christ did not become God from man, but the Word, being God, became flesh, that is, man.

(25) And he is said to have emptied himself, since before the emptying he had the fullness in his own nature, as he is known to be God. For he did not ascend to fullness from

---

[40] Jn 1.14.   [41] Jl 3.1.

being someone empty, but rather he humbled himself from the divine heights and ineffable glory, not by being a humble man who was lifted up by having been glorified. As one free he took the form of a servant. He did not ascend to freedom after being a servant. He who is in the form of[42] and equal to the Father was made in the likeness of men; nor being man was he enriched by participation in regard to being in the likeness of God. Why, therefore, do they reverse the statements of the Incarnation and falsify the truth by rising up against all the divinely inspired Scriptures which know that he is God even after the Son became man and everywhere name him the one Son?

(26) And therefore in the Book of Genesis Moses wrote that the godly Jacob sent his children across the torrent Jabbock and remained alone and a man wrestled with him until the dawn and Jacob called the name of that place, the face of God,[43] for he says, "I have seen God face to face and my life has been spared." "The sun rose on him just as he passed the face of God. And Jacob limped because of his thigh."[44] For by the patriarch God foretold that his only begotten Son would become man at the proper time and would have Israel[45] as his antagonist, and that with regard to him the Israelites would not walk rightly but, as it were, would go lame as he says through the song of the Psalmist, "Strange children have lied to me, strange children have grown old and gone lame from their paths."[46] For this I think is to signify Jacob limping because of his thigh. But consider this, although a man was wrestling with him, he says that he saw God face to face and he called him [the man] the face of God.

(27) For the Son remained the Word of God, although he became man, being the Father in form,[47] according to his spiritual image,[48] I mean, and being in every way unchangeable. And accordingly he said to Philip, revealing himself as "the

[42] Cf. Phil 2.6   [43] Cf. Gn 32.32.
[44] Cf. Gn 32.31–33.
[45] Gn 32.29; Jacob's name was changed to Israel.
[46] Cf. Ps 17.45, 46 (LXX).   [47] Cf. Phil 2.6.
[48] Cf. 2 Cor 4.4 and Col 1.15.

image of the substance"[49] of the Father even in flesh, "He who has seen me has seen the Father."[50] But when he healed the blind man, one of those who was blind from birth, after finding him in the temple, he said, "'Do you believe in the Son of God?' He answered and said, 'Who is he, Lord, that I may believe in him?' And Jesus said to him, 'You have both seen him, and he it is who speaks with you.'"[51] The blind man did not see him bare or without flesh but rather in form like unto us, and he believed in him whom he saw, not as a son connected to another son, but in him who by nature and in truth is not without flesh and who has brought light to men upon the earth. Moreover, the divinely inspired Moses says in the blessings, "Give to Levi his manifestation and to the holy man his truth; whom they tested in a test and reproached at the water of contradiction. He said to his father and to his mother, 'I have not seen you;' he did not acknowledge his brothers."[52]

(28) For the God of all had ordained that the foot-length garment would belong to Aaron, a garment finely woven, and this was a garment proper only to the high priesthood and attributed to it. And on the breast of the high priest were certain stones hanging, twelve in number,[53] in the midst of which were placed two other stones, manifestation and truth.[54] By means of a riddle through these the chorus of the holy apostles is clearly signified being, as it were, in a circle around Emmanuel, who is manifestation and truth, for he manifested the truth by having taken away the worship of God in shadows and in types. But how is it possible to doubt that the only begotten Word of God has become our high priest when he became man since the divinely inspired Paul has written as follows, "Consider the apostle and high priest of our confes-

---

[49] Heb 1.3.   [50] Jn 14.9.
[51] Jn 9.35–38.   [52] Cf. Dt 33.8, 9.
[53] Cf. Ex 28.15–21. Thummim and Urim are referred to in Ex 28.30. They were apparently lots of some kind drawn or cast by the priests to ascertain God's decision in uncertain matters. The burse in which they were kept was called the "breastpiece of decision." Cf. J. Huesman, *JBC* 3:79; J. Castelot, *JBC* 76:8.
[54] Cyril gives the meaning "manifestation and truth" to Thummim and Urim. His objection to the Jewish worship in types and according to the Law is found in other works also, cf. Wilken, *Judaism*, 67, 69–92.

sion, Jesus, who is faithful to him who made him."[55] For the
dignity of the priesthood would rightly be known to be not
unfitting to the measure of his humanity or less than it according to the nature and glory of the Word of God, but not
inharmonious to the Incarnation. For human things have become his. Accordingly he says, "Give to Levi, that is, to the
priest, the manifestation and the truth." To what kind of Levi
or priest did he[56] speak when he said, "To the holy man," for
our Lord Jesus Christ did not commit sin?[57] Therefore, Paul
writes about him, "For it is fitting that we should have a high
priest, holy, innocent, undefiled, set apart from sinners, and
become higher than the heavens."[58] They tested him in a test;
they reproached him at the water of contradiction.[59]

(29) O, unexpected event! By saying he is man, at once he
reveals that he is God, whom Israel irritated and tested both
in the desert and at the water of contradiction. And the Psalmist testifies saying, "He split a rock in the desert and gave them
to drink as in great abundance and he brought forth water
from a rock and he poured forth waters like rivers."[60] And
what does Scripture say after this? They tempted him in their
hearts and ridiculed their God and said, "Will God be able to
provide a table in a desert because he struck a rock and waters
rushed forth and torrents were inundated? Will he be able to
give bread or prepare a table for his people?"[61] Understand,
therefore, how they rant against God who works wonders,
who Moses says is a man. For understanding it thus, the divinely inspired Paul also writes, "For they drank from the
spiritual rock which followed them, but the rock was Christ."[62]
The man, therefore, whom they reproached was he, who when
not yet incarnate, was put to the test by those from Israel. For
Moses, again, has proved by another sign that he was not another son before he was made flesh, and that there was not a
son of the seed of David different from him, as some dare to

[55] Heb 3.1.2.
[56] God speaking through the prophetic mouth of Moses.
[57] Cf. 1 Pt 2.22.   [58] Heb 7.26.
[59] Cf. Dt 33.8   [60] Ps 77 (78).15, 16.
[61] Ps 77 (78).18–20.   [62] 1 Cor 10.4.

say, but one and the same, the still unclothed Word before the Incarnation, and incarnate and made man after the birth from the Holy Virgin, as the holy and divinely inspired Fathers have written.

(30) For as if someone was asking and desired to learn concerning what kind of a man he had mentioned, whom he says was put to the test and reproached by those of Israel, almost by stretching out his hand he indicates Jesus and says, "He who says to his father and his mother, 'I have not seen you,' and did not recognize his own brothers."[63] For we recall that one of the holy evangelists has written that at one time when Christ was teaching and instructing some people, his mother and brethren stood by, and then one of the disciples ran up and said, "Your mother and brethren are standing outside, wishing to see you,"[64] and he, after stretching out his hand over his disciples, said, "My mother and my brethren are they who hear the Word of God and act upon it."[65] "For whoever does the will of my Father in heaven, he is my brother and sister and mother."[66] This, I think, is the same thing which Moses said, "He who says to his father and his mother, 'I have not seen you,' and did not recognize his own brothers." Moreover, the all-wise Daniel says that he saw the only begotten Word of God in form like unto us. He says he saw the ancient of days sitting upon a throne and myriads upon myriads attended him and thousands upon thousands were ministering to him and, after making certain other statements in between, Daniel adds, "As the visions during the night continued, I saw one like the Son of man coming on the clouds of heaven; and when he reached the ancient of days and was presented before him, he received glory and kingship; and all tribes and tongues shall serve him."[67] Behold, again Emmanuel is manifestly and clearly seen ascending to God the Father in heaven. For "a cloud took him"[68] whom he[69] says is not simply a man

[63] Dt 33.9.
[65] Lk 8.21.
[67] Cf. Dn 7.13, 14.
[69] Luke, author of the Acts.
[64] Lk 8.20.
[66] Mt 12.50.
[68] Acts 1.9.

but the Son of man.[70] For he was God the Word made in a likeness unto us. With this understanding the all-wise Paul says that he was "made like unto men"[71] and that he "appeared in the form of man" and that he was found "in the likeness of sinful flesh"[72] by those upon the earth.

(31) But if he was a man honored as God because of a conjunction with God, the prophet Daniel would have said that he saw one coming on the clouds as if God, or as if the Son of God, but he does not say this, but rather he says this, namely, like the Son of man. Therefore he knew that the Son was God and made man, that is, made in the likeness of man, just as Paul says. Yet, although he has appeared in flesh, "he reached the ancient of days,"[73] that is, he ascended to the throne of his eternal Father "and he was given honor and kingship; and all tribes and tongues shall serve him." This certainly was stated by him, "Father, glorify me with the glory that I had with you before the world existed."[74] And, that the incarnate Word of God is sitting with him and is equal in glory to God the Father, and, though he is with flesh, that he is one Son even when he became man, the all-wise Paul makes clear when he writes, "We have such a high priest, who has taken his seat at the right hand of the throne of majesty on high."[75] And indeed our Lord Jesus Christ, when the Jews asked him whether he is in truth the Christ, said, "If I tell you, you will not believe me; and if I question you, you will not answer me. But henceforth, the Son of man will be seated at the right hand of the power of God."[76] Accordingly the chorus of the holy prophets beheld the Son, even incarnate, on the throne of divinity.

(32) Let us see the heralds of the New Testament also, the spiritual teachers of all under the sun, to whom Christ himself said, "It is not you who are speaking, but the Spirit of your Father who speaks through you."[77] We shall, therefore, find the Baptist saying, "After me there comes a man who was be-

[70] Cf. Acts 3.13, 14.
[71] Phil 2.7.
[72] Rom 8.3
[73] Cf. Dn 7.13, 14.
[74] Jn 17.5.
[75] Heb 8.1.
[76] Lk 22.67–69.
[77] Mt 10.20.

fore me because he was first."[78] But how was he before the Baptist, who was coming after the Baptist? How is it not clear to all that Christ existed later than John according to the time of the flesh? What, therefore, might one say to these questions? The Savior has resolved for us what we ask, for he said when speaking to the Jews, "Amen, amen, I say to you, before Abraham came to be, I am."[79] For he was before Abraham as God, but he is known after him insofar as he appeared as man. And then, since God the Father clearly cried out, "My glory I shall not give to another,"[80] for "there is no God besides him,"[81] Christ said to us, "When the Son of man comes with the holy angels in the glory of his Father."[82] Since the Son of man is expected to come down from heaven, again the all-wise Paul writes, "For the grace of God our Savior has appeared to all men, in order that, rejecting ungodliness and worldly lusts, we may live temperately, justly, piously and honestly in this world, looking for the blessed hope and glorious coming of our great God and Savior, Jesus Christ."[83] And elsewhere he said, when making statements about those of the blood of Israel, that they have "the covenant and the legislation and the worship and from them is the Christ according to the flesh, who is over all things, God blessed forever, amen."[84]

(33) Accordingly, following in the footsteps of the confession of the Fathers without deviation we say that the very Word of God the Father, begotten as the only begotten Son, was incarnate, and was made man, suffered, died, and rose from the dead on the third day. The Word of God is impassible confessedly as far as pertains to his own nature as the Word of God. No one is so thunderstruck as to think that the nature which is over all things is able to be receptive of suffering. But because he became man by having made his own the flesh from the Holy Virgin, for this reason we stoutly maintain, following the plans of the Incarnation that he who is God was beyond suffering, suffered in his own flesh as a hu-

[78] Jn 1.30.
[80] Is 42.8
[82] Mk 8.38.
[84] Rom 9.4, 5.

[79] Jn 8.58.
[81] Is 45.5.
[83] Cf. Ti 2.11–13.

man being. If he became man, being God, in no way did he
cease being God. If he became a part of creation, he also remained above creation. If, being legislator as God, he came to
be "under the law,"[85] he was still legislator. If being master according to his divinity, he put on "the form of a slave,"[86] yet he
still has the inseparable dignity of a master. If, being the only
begotten, he became "the firstborn among many brethren,"[87]
and yet is the only begotten, what is the paradox if, although
suffering in the flesh according to his humanity, even so he is
known to be impassible according to his divinity? And so the
all-wise Paul says that the Word himself who is "in the form of
God"[88] and equal to God the Father "became obedient even
unto death, death of the cross."[89]

(34) In another of his own epistles he says about him, "He is
the image of the invisible God, the firstborn of every creature.
For in him were created all things in the heavens and on the
earth. And he is before all creatures, and in him all things
hold together."[90] He says that he is the head of the church,[91]
and is "the first-fruits of those who have fallen asleep"[92] and
"the firstborn of the dead."[93] Yet the Word of God the Father
is life and life-giving since he was begotten of life, that is from
him who begot him. How then did he become the firstborn of
the dead and the first-fruits of those who have fallen asleep?
When he made his own, the flesh which was receptive of death,
"by the grace of God," as the all-wise Paul says, "he tasted
death on behalf of every man,"[94] in his flesh which was able to
suffer without him ceasing to be life. Accordingly, even though
it is stated that he suffered in his flesh, he did not receive the
suffering in the nature of his divinity, but, as I said just now, in
his own flesh which was receptive of suffering. And so the
blessed prophet Isaiah, knowing that God made man suffered
in his flesh, says about him, "Dumb like a lamb he was led before the one who sheared him. He was silent and thus he does

[85] Gal 4.4.   [86] Phil 2.7.
[87] Rom 8.30.   [88] Phil 2.6.
[89] Phil 2.8.   [90] Col 1.15–17.
[91] Col 1.18.   [92] 1 Cor 15.20.
[93] Col 1.18.   [94] Heb 2.9.

not open his mouth. Oppressed and condemned he was taken away, and who shall describe his generation? His life is taken from the land."[95]

(35) But if he was some man and is considered a son separately but conjoined to God, as proponents of impious doctrines pretend, how is it still difficult to find a man able to describe his generation? He was born of the seed of Jesse and of David.[96] But who is the one able to tell the begetting of the Word of God or the manner of the begetting? His life is taken from the land, that is, his existence, for he has laid down his life, but not his existence. He is lifted on high and is borne above those upon the earth,[97] for discussion of that ineffable nature is incomprehensible and totally inaccessible to the understandings of men. I will add these words also to what has been said, "One Lord, one faith, one baptism," as the most holy Paul says.[98] Since, therefore, there is one Lord, one faith, and one baptism, who is the Lord and in whom have we believed and been baptized? But perhaps one might say that it is most fitting that in the Word which is from God the Father is fulfilled the power and the faith which is for us and the saving baptism, for thus he gave commands to his holy apostles saying, "Go, therefore, and make disciples of all nations, baptizing them in the name of the Father, and of the Son, and of the Holy Spirit."[99]

(36) But the divinely inspired Paul renders the glory of his lordship and the confession of the faith and the power of holy baptism clear by saying, "Do not say in your heart: Who shall ascend into heaven? (that is, to bring down Christ); or, Who shall descend into the abyss? (that is, to bring up Christ from the dead). But what does Scripture say? 'The word is near you, in your mouth and in your heart.' For if you confess that Jesus is the Lord, and believe in your heart that God has raised him from the dead, you shall be saved."[100]

(37) And he writes again, "Do you not know that all we who have been baptized into Christ Jesus have been baptized into

[95] Is 53. 7, 8.
[97] Cf. Eph 4.8–10.
[99] Mt 28.18, 19.
[96] Cf. Is 11.1.
[98] Eph 4.5.
[100] Rom 10.6–9.

his death?"[101] Behold Paul clearly places the confession of
lordship and of faith and the very grace of holy baptism de-
pendent upon him who suffered death and rose from the
dead. Therefore, we do not believe in two sons, do we? Shall
we pass over the Word who shone forth from God the Father
and shall we attribute as if to another son different from him,
that is, to the Son who suffered, the glory of lordship, the confession of the faith itself and our heaven-sent baptism? Yet
how is it not stupid, or rather even indubitably impious, to
think or say such things.

(38) What, then, shall we say? "One Lord in truth, one faith
and one baptism."[102] For he is one Son and Lord, not because
the Word assumed a man according to a conjunction and declared him to be a partaker of his own dignities, and communicated to him the filiation and the lordship, as some delirious
men state and write; but because He is the Word of God, light
of light, incarnate and made flesh. We are baptized in the
death of him who suffered in his humanity in his own flesh,
but who has remained impassible in his divinity and lives forever. He is life from the life of God the Father. Thus, death
was conquered, which dared to assault the body of life, and
thus corruption even in us is nullified and the strength of
death itself is weakened, and accordingly Christ said, "Amen,
amen, I say to you, unless you eat the flesh of the Son of man,
and drink his blood, you do not have life in you."[103]

(39) Therefore the holy body and blood of Christ are life-
giving. His body, as I said, is not that of some man who would
be partaker of life, but rather is the very own body of life by
nature, obviously the body of the only begotten. The Christ-
loving chorus of the holy Fathers holds these doctrines with us
and also he who now adorns the throne of the holy Church of
Constantinople, our most holy and most God-fearing brother
and fellow bishop, Proclus.[104] For he himself has written also
to the most God-loving bishops of the East as follows, in these

[101] Rom 6.3.   [102] Eph 4.5.
[103] Jn 6.54.
[104] After the death of Maximian, Proclus, bishop of Cyzicus, an anti-
Nestorian, became Bishop of Constantinople in 434, cf. Quasten 3.521–525.

very words, "And he who is without visible shape is incarnate without change, he who is without beginning is born according to the flesh, he who is all-perfect 'advances in age'[105] according to the body, he who is above suffering endures sufferings, enduring insults not in that which he continued to be but receiving the sufferings of the body in that which he became." Accordingly the bad faith of those who think or write things different from this is proved to be in every way sick with what is profane and discordant with the doctrines of the truth.

(40) After the thrice-blessed Fathers have brought to an end the statement about Christ, they mention the Holy Spirit. For they stated that they believe in him, just as they do in the Father and in the Son. For his is consubstantial with them and he is poured forth, that is, he proceeds as from the fountain of God the Father and he is bestowed on creation through the Son. Wherefore, Christ breathed upon the holy apostles saying, "Receive the Holy Spirit."[106] Therefore God the Spirit is from God[107] and not different from the substance which is highest of all, but is from that substance and in it and is its own.

(41) This, therefore, is the upright and most exact faith of the holy Fathers, that is, the confession of faith. But as Paul says, "the god of this world has blinded the minds of unbelievers that they should not see the light of the gospel of the glory of Christ."[108] Accordingly some, after having ceased to go along the straight path of truth, rush against the rocks, "when they understand neither what they say nor the things about which they make assertion."[109] For after attributing the glory of the filiation only to the Word begotten of God the Father, they say that another son of the seed of David and Jesse has been conjoined to him and has a share in the filiation and of the glory proper to God and of the very indwelling of the

---

Proclus died in 446. Cyril's quotation which follows is listed as Fragment 3 of a letter by Proclus *ad Armenios*, cf. PG 65.888.

[105] Lk 2.52.   [106] Jn 20.22.
[107] Cf. Jn 4.24.   [108] 2 Cor 4.4.
[109] 1 Tm 1.7.

Word and has had almost everything from him, but has nothing at all of his own.

(42) Concerning such men, as I think, the disciples of the Savior have written, "For certain men have stealthily entered in, who long ago were marked out for this condemnation, ungodly men who turn the grace of God into wantonness and disown our only master and Lord, Jesus Christ."[110] But Jesus Christ would rightly be named the Word who has appeared in the form of man. Then let those of the opposition, who do not beg off thinking and stating the doctrines of Nestorius and Theodore from their exceedingly great stupidity, answer to those asking them, "Do you reject the doctrine that the Son of the Holy Virgin is God and the true Son of God the Father because you attribute the suffering to her son alone, and hustle him off from being the Word of God, so that God might not be said to be passible?" For these are the discoveries of their pretense of accuracy and the vulgarity of their thoughts. Therefore let them not name him Christ, that is, the anointed one, separately and apart from him, the Word of God the Father. For just as suffering is foreign to him when he is considered without flesh, so also the anointing is an inharmonious matter and foreign to him, for "God anointed Jesus of Nazareth with the Holy Spirit"[111] but of himself the Word of God is entirely perfect and would not need the anointing through the Holy Spirit. So, deny the dispensation, turn the only begotten away from his love for the world, do not let him be named Christ, the anointed one, by you! Was it not a small thing for him to be made in the measure like unto us? Accordingly, since this is also unworthy of him let no one confess that he became man, so that Christ may say to them also, "You err because you know neither the Scriptures nor the power of God."[112]

(43) Accordingly, let us flee the destructive innovations of those who have chosen to think thus because we consider them enemies of the truth, and let us rather follow the doctrines of

[110] Jude 4.   [111] Acts 10.38.
[112] Mt 22.29.

the holy Fathers and the tradition of the holy apostles and evangelists. It was the incarnate Word himself speaking in them, through whom and with whom may there be to God the Father honor, glory, and power with the Holy Spirit, now, and forever, and unto ages of ages. Amen.[113]

[113] Rv 4.11 and 5.12.

LETTER 56

A letter of Cyril, to Gennadius, a priest and archimandrite.[1]

The strength of your reverence[2] with regard to piety I have known, not just now but I knew it from long ago and I praise it strongly, since your reverence desires to live with such precision. But the dispositions of affairs sometimes force[3] some to be swept a little bit out of reach of what ought to be, in order that they may gain some greater result. For just as they who sail the sea, when a storm is at hand and the ship is in danger, because they are anxious, jettison some cargo for the sake of saving the remainder, so we also, in the circumstances in which it may not be possible to save what is exceedingly precise, overlook some things in order that we may not suffer the loss of the whole.

(2) And I write these words knowing that your reverence has been grieved at our most holy and most God-fearing brother and fellow minister, Proclus the bishop, because he received into communion the Bishop of the Church of Aelia[4] whom the laws of the Church of Palestine do not recognize as their leader. But a hollow love of honor, which has bitterness as its result, tends toward an unbridled longing for action.

---

[1] For the critical text of this letter see Schwartz, *Codex Vaticanus gr. 1431*, p. 17. For another critical text of this letter see Périclès-Pierre Joannou, *Fonti: Fascicolo IX: Discipline générale antique (IVᵉ–IXᵉ s.)*, vol. 2: *Les canons des Pères Grecs*, Pontificia commissione per la redazione del codice di diritto canonico orientale (Grottaferrata [Rome]: Tipografia Italo-Orientale "S. Nilo," 1963), 286–287. Geerard numbers this letter 5356 in *CPG*.

[2] Gennadius, the priest and archmandrite.

[3] Following the text published by Schwartz. Joannou's edition, however, reads, "But the disposition of affairs sometimes forces. . . ."

[4] Aelia Capitolina was the ancient Roman name for Jerusalem.

(3) Therefore, let not your reverence turn away from communion with the most holy and most God-loving bishop, Proclus, for both his holiness and I had one thought in the matter, and the manner of the arrangement was displeasing to none of those who knew the circumstances.

LETTER 57

A letter of Cyril, to Maximus, deacon of Antioch.[1]

LEARNED FROM THE beloved monk Paul[2] that your reverence up to this day refuses communion with the most pious John[3] because there are some in the Church of Antioch who either still think as Nestorius did, or have thought so and perhaps desisted. Accordingly let your clemency estimate whether those who are said to be reconciled are nakedly and shamelessly holding the doctrines of Nestorius and telling them to others, or have had their consciences seared once and are now reconciled after having regretted that by which they were held fast, and are ashamed perhaps to admit their blunder. For it happens that some such experiences occur to those who have been beguiled.

(2) And if you see them now agreeing with the true faith, forget about what has gone by. For we wish to see them denying rather than advocating the baseness of Nestorius in a shameless opinion, and in order not to appear to prize a love of strife let us accept communion with the most pious bishop, John, yielding to him also for prudential reasons, not being too demanding in the use of language with regard to those who repent, for the matter, as I said, requires a great deal of charity.

(3) (But I think that the documents which I dispatched to the most pious bishops, I mean Acacius as well as Rabbula and

---

[1] For the critical text of this letter see Schwartz, *Codex vaticanus gr. 1431*, p. 21. For another critical text of this letter see Joannou, *Fonti*, 2:284–285. Geerard numbers this letter 5357 in *CPG*.
[2] Paul delivered the letter to which this is a reply. Cf. Letter 58.
[3] Bishop of Antioch.

Firmus, have already been sent. If this has not yet happened, please send [them] quickly.) [4]

---

[4] The last two sentences are included in p. 21 of Schwartz's text. Joannou did not include them on p. 285 of the text which he published, but mentioned in the *apparatus criticus* that Schwartz had added them.

LETTER 58

To the same.[1]

ETTERS FROM YOUR reverence[2] were delivered again by the beloved monk, Paul, and I was delighted reading them and I observed that your zeal is even now unwearied, which you always had for the true faith, which you also now have and will have in the future, for it is written, "Let him who has begun a good work in you bring it to perfection."[3] When the most pious presbyter Presentinus reached me and explained some things, I wrote what was proper to the most pious and God-fearing bishop, John, and to the archimandrites whom he wished. Your reverence will know the meaning of what I wrote by reading the letters themselves.

(2) However, I say this, that it was the task of your piety not to receive any of those who had a faltering intention either into communion or into the love which is in Christ. The nature of the negotiations now on foot sometimes compels us against our will to be content with what is beside both our intention and opinion. I see at a glance that the most pious bishop, John, himself has need of much charity, in order that he may win those who are rebellious. Often harsh collisions repel those who have been disgraced, and it is better to rescue those who were opponents by gentleness rather than to hurt them with the spareness of precision. Just as if their bodies were ill, it would doubtless be necessary of course to stretch out a hand to them, so since their souls are in pain there is a need of much charity as if it were a medicine being furnished

---

[1] For the critical text of this letter see Schwartz, *Codex vaticanus gr. 1431*, pp. 20–21. Geerard numbers this letter 5358 in *CPG*.
[2] Maximus, a deacon at Antioch.   [3] Cf. Phil 1.6.

for them. Little by little they will themselves come to a sincere disposition and these are the "services of help and power of administration"[4] which the blessed Paul named.

(3) Let not your reverence, therefore, be disturbed, and do not view with extreme precision the negotiations now being conducted especially in the present crisis. We do not desire to cut but to tie following the words of our Savior, "It is not the healthy," he says, "who need a physician, but they who are sick."[5] And if so, as he says again, "I have not come to call the just, but sinners to repentance."[6]

[4] 1 Cor 12.28.   [5] Lk 5.31.
[6] Lk 5.32.

LETTER 59[1]

Y LORD, THE most religious bishop, Beronicianus[2] wrote to me that the pious decree of the emperors, the friends of God, has been given to your excellency,[3] by which decree it is commanded that all the most holy bishops of the East anathematize the impious Nestorius, this is to name the Simonian or Nestorian heresy, I think, and nothing else. The decree signified that all these bishops should be prepared to free their convictions or opinions from such a suspicion because in every way they are free from those blasphemies. Since I desire to strengthen the peace which was granted to the churches by Christ, I pray that all may have this intention and may be free from the innovations of the words of Nestorius.

(2) However, because they say that we ought to seek nothing more beyond what the imperial and holy letters contain, and they ask this of your goodness, deign, in order to help the good opinion of all, to prepare them to anathematize Nestorius and his polluted teachings, to consider him deposed, believing that our one Lord Jesus Christ is, to be sure, the only begotten Son of God, his Word made man and made flesh, not to be divided into two sons, but that he was ineffably begotten from God before all time and in recent periods of time he was born according to the flesh from a woman, so that his person is one also. In this way we know that the Holy Virgin is the Mother of God, because he is God and man at the same time, that he who without change and without confusion is the only begotten, is incarnate and made man, and moreover

---

[1] For the critical text of this letter see Schwartz, *ACO* 1.4 p. 206. Geerard numbers this letter 5359 in *CPG*.

[2] Bishop of Tyre in Phoenicia.

[3] Aristolaus, the secretary and tribune, to whom the letter is addressed.

that he was able to suffer according to the nature of his humanity. We know that it is impossible for him to suffer according to the nature of his divinity, and that he did suffer in his own flesh according to the Scriptures.

(3) When these bishops have been joined together for the anathema against Nestorius, every accusation on other matters, as I think, will be void and the minds of men will be cleansed. Then those who are in the cities will not be in conflict with each other any longer or be at all scandalized at something in their masters because they confess the true and blameless faith which we all keep in us.

(4) I have written these words to my lord, the bishop Beronicianus also. Yet I think that the force of the imperial decrees has the same intent and we would add nothing to what has been ordered by them.

LETTER 60[1]

ALL, NOT ONLY the zealous bishops who are in the great city of Alexandria, but also the most holy bishops throughout all Egypt, have learned of the force of the holy decrees which recently were sent to your excellency.[2] We have offered most intense prayers to God for his gifts, for the victory and endurance of the friends of Christ and of our most religious emperors and may it come about that they be powerful against their enemies and strong against every force resisting them so that we may exist in peace and happiness. This is worthy of the zeal of your excellency.

(2) It was fitting that this decree be committed to your care, for you are such a man, and you intend much that is holy and have a fervent zeal, I mean, for piety and blameless faith. I was praying that all the most holy bishops in the East might not be suspect first of all in any way of the evil opinions of Nestorius but that their very hearts would have had sincere thoughts free of all evil. Thus "rightly handling the word of truth"[3] most uprightly they would have been clothed with a proper care.

(3) But, as I learn, some anathematize the madness of Nestorius only so far as the tongue is concerned and speech, but again dare both to think and say what is his teaching. It is unbelievable if there would be in any respect whatever such men among those to whom the priesthood has been granted. Because there is much whispering together and the persons testifying these matters are not to be despised, but rather are worthy of all reverence, may your goodness deign that you,

---

[1] For the critical text (only the Latin is extant) of this letter see Schwartz, *ACO* 1.4 p. 230. Geerard numbers this letter 5360 in *CPG*.

[2] Aristolaus, the secretary and tribune.

[3] 2 Tm 2.15.

who should be commended to God, see to it with rather atten-
tive care that those especially who are under the suspicion of
this evil anathematize the condemned Nestorius because of
his many blasphemies.

(4) He[4] not only said this, namely, that the Holy Virgin was
not the Mother of God, but added other defenses of the lie
besides these words in opposition to the true and apostolic
tradition. He named two christs as sons, one separately the
Word of God the Father, and another separately besides him;
one from the seed of David and the one whom he called the
instrument of divinity and made divisions in every direction,
and, as it were, forgot the blessed Paul saying, "one Lord, one
faith, one baptism."[5] We have not been baptized into God and
man as into two sons through a difference but in one Christ,
that is, the only begotten Word of God, made man and incarnate, so that he is at the same time God and man, begotten
indeed of the unbegotten God the Father, and likewise born
from the Holy Virgin according to the flesh.

(5) Let your excellency, therefore, not endure those who
have other opinions and babble in vain there. Our Lord Jesus
Christ is one, as I said, and his person is one, incarnate, the
person of him who is by nature and in truth the Son.

(6) Moreover, we state that he is impassible according to his
divinity, but that he suffered in his own flesh according to the
Scriptures. We state that those sufferings which happened to
his flesh are his whose very own body it is. Therefore, he is
impassible according to divinity, but in his own flesh he suffered on our account and for us. And in this way he is pro-
claimed to have come back to life in such a way that, since God
gives life to his very own flesh united to himself, we, too, in
him become more powerful than both death and corruption.

(7) If, however, they anathematize Nestorius in speech and
tongue and yet have other opinions, let them behold hanging
over them peril from God and the outcome pronounced by
the entire council which met at Ephesus. It defined that those

[4] The guilty one is not named. It seems to be Nestorius.
[5] Eph 4.5.

who say and think the teachings which are those of Nestorius,
whether they be bishops or clerics, should be suspended from
their priesthoods; and let them not say that they do not know
the synod which met at Ephesus, so that we may not deny
them and ourselves, as if we did not know that we are bishops.

LETTER 61[1]

T O DESIRE PEACE is a supreme and excellent good. And I[2] say that those who wish to hold opinions pleasing to Christ should abide in this zeal without ceasing and with bravery. However, it is not proper for this reason to despise the virtue of goodness in Christ. But it is most injurious to be overawed and another thing to love peace indeed and the benefits that flow from it. But it is most injurious to bring forth, not those things whereby peace is strengthened and becomes undisturbable, but rather those things which destroy and overturn it and do not permit those matters to remain concerning which peace has been made. I write these words in very great sorrow, for some of the most pious bishops there are said to anathematize Nestorius and his most insane teachings and are trying again, as if from a transformation, to say and think those teachings which are his and to ruin the consciences of their brethren for whom Christ died.

(2) Moreover, I am in wonderment as to how, since they are wise, it escapes them that, if they hold the opinions which they reject, they are anathematizing themselves. For it will be said fittingly, and this is stated in truth, even though it seems burdensome, that they who, I do not know how, are daring to say what are the teachings of Nestorius, clearly state, "I did not anticipate it."[3] And I desire to be slow to believe in such instances considering the extent of the evil. May your holiness, however, deign, if there are still any such as these, to warn

---

[1] For the critical text (only the Latin is extant) of this letter see Schwartz, *ACO* 1.4 p. 207. Geerard numbers this letter 5361 in *CPG*.

[2] A letter of Cyril to John to Antioch.

[3] Evidently signifying that they did not foresee the condemnation and anathema.

and confound them, and stop them from thinking and speaking of the innovations of Nestorius.

(3) How do they anathematize them or how do they desire peace to last when they fight against it and overturn it as a wicked peace? Indeed it was enough in the case of suspected men for them only to anathematize the impious Nestorius and his teachings or blasphemies against Christ.

(4) But since it is likely that some mock this action and say, "He was deposed for this reason, namely, because he would not admit she was the Mother of God and nothing else," I think that it must be said that this statement was not the only cause of his deposition, but also the other very many statements of his which lifted a weapon against the dogmas of truth.

(5) Therefore, it is proper to profess that they anathematize Nestorius and his profane and insane teachings and consider him deposed because they believe that our Lord Jesus Christ is the one and only begotten Son of God.

LETTER 62

Cyril, to John of Antioch.[1]

JUST NOW MOST gladly received the letter full of great rejoicing sent by your excellency. For what is good, what is pleasant, unless brothers dwell in harmony,[2] through unanimity and the same good will in Christ, joined in charity to one another, with the scandals taken from their midst which were introduced, I do not know how, which by the grace of the Savior were extinguished through your holiness once, and moreover will be extinguished in the remaining instances. And this is, I think, what was said by God through the voice of the prophet, "Pass through my gates, clear the stones from this highway."[3]

(2) May it, therefore, happen that all are honoring what are better things, or now at least are ceasing to fight against the truth, and although they favored the vain language of Nestorius, let them now accept the true and blameless word of faith. And these men, who were once called to this, have indeed filled us with very great rejoicing, as I said. And may the God of all grant to your excellency to know how to win over those who have been brought to peace by prayers and instruction which is useful.

(3) But if some contend savagely, they will not blame the mercy of the church, but drawing upon themselves what they are about to suffer they will hear from you, "Walk by the light of your fire and by the brands you have kindled."[4] For it is fitting now to fight the perverse not with gentleness.

[1] For the critical text (only the Latin is extant) of this letter see Schwartz, *ACO* 1.4 pp. 228–229. Geerard numbers this letter 5362 in *CPG*.
[2] Cf. Ps 132(133).1.   [3] Cf. Is 62.10.
[4] Is 50.11.

LETTER 63

Cyril, to John of Antioch against Theodoret.[1]

 PRESUMED THAT the most pious Theodoret along with the other God-fearing bishops had wiped from his hands the stain of the innovations of Nestorius. For I was of the opinion that, once he had written and embraced the peace, and accepted in reply my letter addressed to him, he himself had put out of the way by agreement whatever seemed to stand as an obstacle. But as the most pious priest, Daniel, imparts to me, he exerted himself this far without changing the opinions he held in the beginning, but he holds the blasphemies of that Nestorius, and he plainly is as if he neither anathematized him, nor came forth to sign his deposition.

(2) And let your holiness grant me freedom to speak since I speak out of love; for what reason are some so stiff-necked as not to follow the admirable aim of your reverence, not even in matters of charity, but are like those who forsake the herd and are firm in what seems best to them alone? And yet, if what I learned is true, the most God-fearing man mentioned above ought to gain the experience of the spurs of your reverence.

---

[1] For the critical text of this letter see Schwartz, *Codex vaticanus gr. 1431*, p. 15. Geerard numbers this letter 5363 in *CPG*.

LETTER 64

Cyril, to Maximus, John and Thalassius, priests and archimandrites.[1]

INDEED THE ZEAL of your piety is remarkable and your fervor is full of all praise, for you are zealous "being fervent in the zeal of God"[2] as it is written, in order that Nestorius might not even now say that he is honored by those who think as he does; "I looked for sympathy, but there was none; for comforters, and I found none."[3] And those who resist the dogmas of religion or the worship of God, "kick against the goad"[4] and injure their own souls by offending against Christ and amusing themselves in calumnies against him. But it is foreign to the soul of a bishop to whom it has been allotted to preside over the people, to anathematize with the tongue the polluted and poisoning teachings of Nestorius, but to have a mind filled with them and to overturn the souls of their brethren for whom Christ died.

(2) Therefore, I have written also to my lord the most admirable tribune and secretary, Aristolaus, what your piety would surely write. And I wrote to some others also. But you will know this from the most reverend priest and archimandrite, Adamantius, whose character, way of life, and learning I have admired along with his intellect and rectitude concerning the faith, and, as it were, I beheld you all in him alone.

(3) Since, however, many of the orthodox and most religious bishops have written what is opposed to themselves and to the people who are under their hands, because of the

[1] For the critical text (only the Latin is extant) of this letter see Schwartz, *ACO* 1.4 p. 229. Geerard numbers this letter 5364 in *CPG*.
[2] Cf. 1 Mc 2.54 and 1 Kgs (3 Kgs) 19.10, 14.
[3] Ps 68 (69).21.   [4] Acts 26.14.

insane Nestorians, collecting these matters together I have written a short book concerning the Incarnation of the only begotten, as it were reducing to three chapters all the statements concerning the faith. And the first chapter is that the Holy Virgin is the Mother of God. The second is that Christ is one, and not two. The third is that the Word of God while remaining impassible suffered in his own flesh for us.

(4) Therefore let your piety make arrangements that it be read by the orthodox, for it will be pleasant, I think, for you to have every objection of theirs solved. Do not be remiss in offering prayers for me, for the great pressure of affairs pouring in on all sides is like the unbearable tumult of the waves. Yet I also believe that through the prayers of your piety there will again be tranquillity and peace in Christ.

LETTER 65

Cyril, to Mosaeus, Bishop of Antaradus.[1]

INDEED I HAVE never ceased to write to your reverence and to accept letters directed to me by you. But the issues which have been raised in these matters have become the reason for silence for you and me, and may God grant that this may completely cease and be removed from between us. Some desire difficulties which erect a hedge of separation between us, so that our affection for each other may not be strong enough to unite us. For those who are with the most pious archimandrite, Maximus, have disturbed me very much by writing some things which pertain to the utmost blasphemy and saying that they had been said to them by your reverence.

(2) But we must [approach God] purely since he knows our hearts thoroughly and it is not fitting that with our tongue only we profess the condemnation of the polluted teachings of Nestorius but hold something else in our mind. And I write these words without strongly believing in what was said to me, but desiring to strengthen the opinion of your reverence. But I was very much pleased when I saw what was written by your reverence and delivered through my lord, your most beloved son, Thomas.

[1] For the critical text (only the Latin is extant) of this letter see Schwartz, *ACO* 1.4 p. 231. Geerard numbers this letter 5365 in *CPG*. Antaradus is a town on the coast of Syria, opposite Aradus, an island city.

LETTER 66

To the God-loving and most holy bishop Cyril. John of Antioch and the God-loving bishops from every province in the East meeting by the grace of God in the Christ-loving city of Antioch because of a letter of the most holy bishop, lord Proclus, send greetings.[1]

ROCLUS[2] WROTE THAT we are neglecting what he said to the Armenians. . . .[3] Because of the festivity of the holy and gloriously victorious martyrs, the Maccabees, we unanimously salute our beloved fellow bishop and a bishop[4] sharing your dignity, most God-loving person. In a time of mutual suffering we assume also a common bond in our distress which good men have caused us and all, as it appears, everywhere in the churches of Christ since the Church of Christ is one in the whole world. We always wish that these men, as I have persuaded them by your promises, be shown to belong to us and to be joined to the universal body of the church. We do not wish, however, to say anything to your venerable person that is contrary to this. You are a man of such prudence that you need no one to instruct you in such matters. While you may be at a distance, you see each one and regard him no less than those who are present.

(2) However, let us come to the issue itself. Evils are afoot

[1] For the critical text (only the Latin is extant) of this letter see Schwartz, *ACO* 1.5 p. 310–315. Geerard numbers this letter 5366 in *CPG*.

[2] Proclus became Bishop of Constantinople after Maximian died in 434. See Quasten 3.521–525.

[3] There is a lacuna. The beginning of the letter is lost. Seven letters of Proclus which deal with the Nestorian controversy have survived. Of these the second is addressed to the Armenians and is commonly known as the *Tomus ad Armenios*. For the critical edition see Schwartz, *ACO* 4.2 (1914) pp. 187–195.

[4] The Latin text suggests that an Egyptian bishop had come for the festivities.

and are increasing, and this is the case because of the slow reconciliation, which God has given the world through your holiness and through us your adherents. For behold, while they
are already meeting with all in general, you have checked the
evils by having recourse to a letter to the God-loving and illustrious tribune Aristolaus. You have checked the excesses of
the propositions which they are inventing in their depravity
for the benefit of the supporters of Nestorius, so that we may
thus say that you have, by your letter, quenched the conflagra-
tion which was hoped for and with all speed you have ended
the disturbance in your willingness to help as an excellent
physician who knows how to cure the sufferings of the church.

(3) Now, however, these very same men, as if rising from
sleep, have arrived at the royal city[5] and by disturbing it have
troubled the peace of the church as much as is in them. For
when the most holy bishop Proclus was sending to us the
tome[6] which he wrote to the Armenians, a truly correct and
pious work, and was asking our agreement, everything was
done by us and we have left nothing undone. Moreover, at the
present time this was even superfluous, because by the grace
of God now all men everywhere hold one and the same holy
opinion. For sometimes matters which seem necessary in some
way, if they are not done at the right time, are accustomed to
produce an increase of confusion.

(4) There is also another evil more monstrous in hostility.
They have another volume having certain excerpts of blessed
Theodore, who was bishop of Mopsuestia, and things which
he seems to have said in different books, and they wish to impose an anathema on them. For this reason we ask that you
apply your mind to us more zealously than in other matters
and deign to consider that this task of theirs is evil, unless
from our common opinion you labor to extinguish it. For God
gave you, besides the will, also the ability, so that you help all
in common. There are in that volume some statements that
are uncertain and are able to be understood in a different

---

[5] Constantinople. Who these persons were is left obscure by the lacuna.
[6] This is the *Tomus ad Armenios*, Letter 2 of Proclus, an answer to the *capitula*
sent to Proclus by the Armenian monks. See Quasten 3.414, 524.

sense than they have been stated. We also admit this, that we see very many of them are open and correct without ambiguity. But there are many like these which are considered obscure and we find them said by very many of his predecessors and the glorious Fathers. And there lurks no small danger that among them we cancel the sayings of the Fathers while refuting the words of that man[7] who, when performing the duties of the episcopate, was adorned with ten thousand victories in his struggle against the Arians, Eunomians, and other heretics through all his life.

(5) But if this is done, we would be about to retract and repudiate many things also openly said by other holy Fathers, for we find certain statements similar to those excerpts in the thrice-blessed and noble Athanasius,[8] some also in the blessed Basil, and some in both blessed Gregories. Many also have been often stated in the writings of Amphilochius,[9] and not a few also in our common father, the blessed Theophilus.[10] For there are some which your holiness confesses in the same way also and has the same opinion. There are also by the God-loving Proclus himself some statements in the very same tome which he sent to the Armenians[11] in which in many senses he agrees with those excerpts. Time will run out for us going through the others: blessed Eustathius, Bishop of Antioch[12] who was given a place of honor for the true faith at the Council of Nicaea, and your own Alexander of great renown,[13] and after those most holy bishops, Meletius[14] and Flavian,[15] by whom many things were said which agree with these statements.

(6) Now what shall we say about these men who have been

---

[7] Theodore of Mopsuestia.

[8] For details of the writings of these Fathers mentioned see the following: On Athanasius, see Quasten 3.72–76; on Basil, see Quasten 3.204–35; on Gregory of Nazianzus, see Quasten 3.236–54; and on Gregory of Nyssa, see Quasten 3.254–96.

[9] Bishop of Iconium. See Quasten 3.296–300.

[10] Predecessor and uncle of Cyril. Most of his writings are lost. See Quasten 3.100–106.

[11] See note 6.   [12] See Quasten 3.302–6.

[13] Alexander of Alexandria. See Quasten 3.13–19.

[14] Meletius, Bishop of Antioch. See Quasten 3.3, 14, 207, 278, 424.

[15] Flavian, Bishop of Antioch. See Quasten 3.103, 401, 425.

honored in the West as following the same doctrine and the
same confession, whom your holiness also has known rather
well? Look, therefore, I ask you, to what a precipice they, who
strive with words to no good, are driving us. What is there
that is full of injury, corruption and confusion that would not
be generated by this, if a door should be opened to those who
wish to overthrow the sayings of the dead Fathers?What damage will it not be, if their words are not only refuted but also
anathematized? For indeed that one thing should be pleasing
to sober and ecclesiastical reason and another should not be
pleasing in the sayings of some persons whether they are ancient, or later, or even our own, that is one matter. However,
we think it appears bold and harsh to impose an anathema
upon them, even though they would not be anathematized
personally along with their statements. For which of us would
not expect to be deposed, or by whom has something not
been said which someone could stir up, or what one of these
would not always furnish an occasion so that the people would
be disturbed? And this, in truth, both for the living and for
those now dead, is a usual thing to happen; but we say this not
only to one who does not know but also to the one who can see
the magnitude of this absurdity more than all of us.

(7) Moreover, what desirable thing would we not offer as a
result of this to the defenders of Nestorius? For who will not
honor him, if others also, who have laid down their lives in the
episcopacy, are anathematized with him at the same time? Or
where will his reputation not be increased by this? And which
of those deceived men, by seizing their chance from this, will
not call Nestorius a confessor, as if the sufferings he endured
on their account are the sufferings which they endured who
have shone in the church?

(8) Moreover, which of those who have understanding does
not know that what was spoken harshly by blessed Theodore,
was said when he was driven by necessity? For the entire East
in common, of those who were before us, proposed him as a
man having great strength of learning against heresies and,
when fighting and struggling against these, he used a certain

great distinction,[16] not coming to it from a depraved understanding, but deciding to use that mode of expression more
efficaciously against the heretics, and he was not ignoring or
denying the total unity, far from it, for all his books are full of
this mode of expression, but he was dividing the properties of
the natures more fully as the fight which he had against the
heretics dictated that he should do.

(9) Your holiness settled this also clearly in your previous
letter to the satisfaction of some of our venerable fellow bishops, and this itself is fitting to your virtue and your wisdom.
In this letter you said that you were resisting the numerous
vanities of Nestorius.[17] For the ears of some men are accustomed to be frightened by the opinions of others and in fact
many such things cause contradictions.

(10) And so we have hastened of necessity to inform your
wisdom after God, so that you would hasten your aid. And we
ourselves need the assistance of fraternal help and of a right
hand accustomed to repel the on-going disturbances of calumny. For we know and are convinced that there is nothing
left of sorrow or weakness of spirit in that holy soul of yours,
for you know thoroughly how to delineate in the dark those
same things which fought in the dark. But strengthen your
good will also at that time, we ask, and show that it is proper to
examine what is common to all the churches, and may your
letter swiftly come to the most holy bishop Proclus, asking
that he avoid the novelties which are in motion against us and
that he would work to preserve the peace which has come to
be also among us and manifest undisturbed zeal to us against
such diabolical machinations, lest in the present time that
prophecy be fulfilled, "Peace, peace, and there will not be
peace."[18]

(11) For behold, they were considering a schism of the
people as a result of the disturbance, until we satisfied them,

---

[16] The distinctions between the two natures in Christ. See Quasten 3.415–18.
[17] Schwartz refers to *Collectio Casinensis*, Letter 145.8. See *ACO* 1.4 pp.
96–97.
[18] Cf. Jer 6.14 and 8.11.

because something unsuitable had not been said or done by
the assembled synod against the teachers mentioned before.[19]
Now, appeasing the tumult of the people, we believe also that
your holiness heeds us, and so we have written a synodical
letter to you, in which we have accepted the volume previously
sent to us,[20] and we have rejected those who have dared by ad-
ditions or by deletions to corrupt the faith which was defined
at Nicaea by our holy and most blessed Fathers, and we confess that our Lord, Jesus Christ, is the one only begotten Son
of God. For thus we know the differences and the properties
of the natures but nevertheless the supreme and inseparable
unity; and at the same time we think that those who introduce
a duality of sons or christs are alien from the true faith and we
embrace that holy saying of your reverence, which stated in
agreement with the Holy Scriptures, "One Lord, Jesus Christ,
although the difference of the natures is not ignored."

(12) Therefore, knowing the [wisdom][21] of your holy excellency we ask [of you as] one body that you hasten to bring
your zeal to bear on the common sufferings of the church, so
that nothing hereafter may be set in motion which is able to
cause disturbances after this unity which came to be, not without the grace of God, in all the churches of the world.

---

[19] Athanasius, Basil, and the other Fathers mentioned earlier.
[20] Schwartz refers to *Collectio Casinensis*, Letters 286 and 287. See *ACO* 1.4
pp. 208–10.
[21] Schwartz emended a lacuna here: *sapientiam, ab ea sicut.*

LETTER 67

Cyril, to John of Antioch and the synod assembled there.[1]

HE DRAGON, THE deserter, truly the most difficult beast fighting against God, has not rested nor has he desisted ever from the peevishness which is in him, but being in labor with the incessant hatred which is in him for the holy churches, he has dared to raise up against the dogmas of the truth, somehow, the impotent tongues of unholy and profane men who "have their consciences branded."[2] But he is conquered everywhere and he has been defeated, since Christ, the Savior of us all, reveals that the perversity and force of his undertakings do nothing.

(2) Accordingly, there were very many men before our time who, having fought against our holy Fathers and having borne the arms of their impudent loquacity against his ineffable glory, were yet proved to be rash, and ignorant, and vainly talking rather than knowing anything in truth of those things which the very truth testifies are true, as they are blameless and higher than any calumny.

(3) But when after them the inventor and teacher of every impiety raised "the profane novelties"[3] of Nestorius against us, behold we all, through the grace of God and the understanding given to us by him, anathematize, with one voice, the apostate, following the footsteps of the glorious zeal of the Fathers, being manly against the enemies of the cross of Christ, honoring the true faith, and teaching in the churches not to agree with the blasphemies of those men saying that there are two christs and sons, one by nature and true, the Word of God

---

[1] For the critical text of this letter see Schwartz, *ACO* 1.1.4 p. 37–39. Geerard numbers this letter 5367 in *CPG*.
    [2] 1 Tm 4.2.   [3] 1 Tm 6.20.

the Father, the other by adoption and grace the one from the seed of David; but, according to the pure and blameless faith which came down to us from the beginning, one Son and Lord Jesus Christ, the Word of God the Father made man and incarnate according to the confession of the holy Fathers so that the same one is and is said to be divine from God the Father as his Word and by nature to proceed from his substance, and is from the seed of David according to the flesh, that is, from Mary the holy Mother of God.

(4) For they "who from the beginning were eye-witnesses and ministers of the word"[4] did not hand on to us that he was one Son and another, as I said, but one and the same, God and man at the same time, the only begotten and the first-born, in order that he might have the first title as God, and the second as man, when he "was born among many brethren"[5] having assumed likeness to ourselves and not having joined another man to himself, as it seemed good to some persons to think, but really and truly becoming man and not relinquishing being what he was. For being God by nature and impassible, for this reason he voluntarily suffered in his own flesh. For he has not given the body of some one else for us, but the only begotten Word of God himself offered himself, after he became man, as an immaculate victim to God the Father.

(5) Therefore it was necessary for us to hold a brilliant festival for those reasons, since plainly there has been cast out along with the evil teachings of Nestorius every other voice from anywhere if it agrees with his lying words. For what we and your holiness unchangeably said proceeded against all those who think the same as he, or even those who have ever thought so, namely, that we anathematize those speaking of two sons and of two christs. For, as I said, by us ourselves and by you one Christ and Son and Lord is preached, the only begotten Word of God "being made like unto men and appearing in the form of man"[6] according to the saying of the very wise Paul.

4 Lk 1.2.   6 Phil 2.7.
5 Cf. Rom 8.29.

(6) And it has been demonstrated in many places that we state that the flesh of the Lord is animated by a rational soul and in his letter to the Armenians[7] by rightly expounding the word of truth our most holy and most God-fearing brother and fellow bishop, Proclus, wisely preached. For he is a pious man and one who practiced to contest those who "cast aside what is right,"[8] since it is his custom to win the victory when preaching the truth.

(7) Let no one attribute, we beg you, discredited opinions, I mean those of Diodore and Theodore[9] or of some others, whom it were better not to praise in order that I might not say something vulgar, and their bearing down on the glory of Christ as if with full sails; let no one attribute these to our holy and orthodox Fathers, I mean, Athanasius, Basil, the Gregories, Theophilus, and the others, lest the matter somehow become an occasion of scandal to some, because they thought that truly the guardians of all orthodox thought had taught in this fashion, and not that they raised up in opposition the books put forth not only against the evil teachings of Nestorius but also against those of others, who have thought and written the teachings of Nestorius before him. But we pray that all are tending to their own affairs and are not causing disturbances in the churches, and that all who are now bringing harmony by the grace of Christ and through the restraint of the teachers everywhere do not hoe up these matters to their detriment or that of others.

(8) But it is necessary for those, who at one time held the teachings of Nestorius, after having changed their minds according to truth, and departing from his nonsense, and changing over to desiring to choose the blameless faith, to be receptive and not to cast reproaches because of what is past, lest somehow this might produce an occasion for delay to some "striving after better gifts."[10] For if we pray that those in physi-

---

[7] This is extant among the *Letters* of Proclus, cf. PG 65.855 and Cyril's Letter 66, note 6.

[8] Cf. Mi 3.9.

[9] Diodore of Tarsus and Theodore of Mopsuestia, teachers of Nestorius.

[10] Cf. 1 Cor 12.31.

cal illnesses be freed from them, and we have pleasure with them when this happens to them, how would one not much more rejoice when the one who has wandered turns back and with a good conscience rushes toward the light of knowledge of the truth. For that it is customary for even the angels to hold celebration in these instances,[11] your holiness knows, since you teach this and preach it in all the churches, for you are not ignorant of the words of our Savior.

(9) We, however, urge you, as brothers and fellow teachers, to command the clerics not to say anything else especially in the churches except true and approved doctrines and those which are judged to be good and to follow rather the confession of the true faith, and especially not to run after discussions concerning these subjects. But, if there may be a necessity somehow because of the need to instruct some in divine mysteries, in no way permit the discussion about the faith to wander off from the truth. But since it is necessary that the occasion of disturbances be cut off by the restraint of your holiness we have written this, which we thought is good.

(10) If, therefore, some either of the clerics or of the monks are accused by some to the effect that they are in communion with the church but up to that point held the teachings of the impious Nestorius, let a hearing be provided for them in the churches rather, and, before you who guide them, let a precise examination be made of what they say. For it is likely that those who desire to make accusations would cause trouble in the courts outside, since no one would allow the statements by them to be admitted. It is also better by far, and more just, to deal with and define ecclesiastical questions in the churches and not before some others by whom a decision in these matters would be entirely inharmonious.

(11) Salute the brotherhood with you. That with us salutes you in the Lord.

[11] Cf. Lk 15.10.

LETTER 68

Of the same, to Acacius of Melitene, Theodotus [of Ancyra and Firmus of Caesarea.][1]

T WAS NOT fitting that it escape the notice of your holiness and, perhaps, you may have already also learned, that all the holy bishops of the East came to Antioch, since my lord, the most holy bishop Proclus, directed a volume to them full of good thoughts and true teachings. Indeed, it was a great and long discussion concerning the dispensation of our Lord Jesus Christ. To it were appended some *Capitula*[2] excerpted from the books of Theodore, which had a meaning suited to the evil teachings of Nestorius, and Proclus urged that it be anathematized by them.[3] They, however, did not permit it.

(2) Then they wrote to me,[4] because, if it happened that the writings of Theodore be anathematized, this stain would run everywhere even to our holy Fathers, I mean indeed Athanasius, Basil, Gregory, Theophilus and the rest. "For they themselves wrote," they say, "also things which are in agreement with Theodore." It was necessary to write to them, and not in uncertain terms, things which the most reverend priest, Daniel, will make known to your holiness. He happened to arrive at Alexandria and has known thoroughly one after the other the matters which have been set in motion.

[1] For the critical text (only the Latin is extant) on which this letter is based see Schwartz, *ACO* 1.4 p. 231–232. Another critical text can be found in Schwartz, *ACO* 4.1 pp. 86–87. Geerard numbers this letter 5368 in *CPG*. Schwartz notes in *ACO* 1.4 that a copy of the letter to Acacius was sent by Cyril to Theodotus and Firmus. Caesarea is in Cappadocia.

[2] These were not in the Letter of Proclus to the Armenians. The title is that of the first collection of abstracts from Theodore of Mopsuestia, cf. Quasten 3.414.

[3] Cf. Letter 66, note 6.   [4] Cf. Letter 66.

65

LETTER 69

Of the same Cyril, to Acacius of Melitene.[1]

THE MOST PIOUS and most God-loving deacon and archimandrite, Maximus, came to me. I gazed upon him, the sort of man as one would likely wait for a long time to meet. I marveled at his zeal and rectitude, and the urge he has toward piety in Christ. He was so distressed and had a mind so full of anxieties that he was gladly willing to endure any toil for the sake of tearing out by the roots the evil teaching of Nestorius from the districts of the East. He read to me the letter of your holiness written to John, the most God-loving Bishop of Antioch, a letter full of much confidence and love of God.

(2) I have written also such a letter to him, but, as it seems, the worse is winning. While feigning to hate the teachings of Nestorius they weld them together again in a different way by admiring the teachings of Theodore although they are tainted with an equal, or rather a far worse, impiety. For Theodore was not the pupil of Nestorius, but Nestorius was his, and they speak as if from one mouth spitting up one poison of heterodoxy from their hearts. The bishops of the East, accordingly, wrote to me that it was not necessary to discredit the teachings of Theodore, in order that, they say, those of the blessed Athanasius, Theophilus, Basil, and Gregory might not also be discredited. For they, too, said what Theodore said.

(3) I did not endure them writing these things, but I said with frankness that Theodore had both a blasphemous tongue and a pen that served it, while they have been teachers of

---

[1] For the critical text of this letter see Schwartz, *Codex vaticanus gr. 1431*, pp. 15–16. Geerard numbers this letter 5369 in *CPG*.

complete orthodoxy and were eminent for this. But they so convinced those in the East that outcries occurred in the churches on the part of the people, "Let the faith of Theodore increase. As Theodore believed, so we believe," although they once hit him with stones when he ventured to say something brief before them in the church. But as the teacher desires, so the flock thinks. I, therefore, neither ceased reproving what he had written nor shall I cease.

(4) Since it was necessary that written opposing arguments be present before them, after looking into the books of Theodore and Diodore[2] in which they had written, not about the Incarnation of the only begotten, but rather against his Incarnation, I selected certain of the chapters and in the approved manner I set myself against them revealing that their teaching was in every way full of abomination. And when the most pious deacon and archimandrite, Maximus, mentioned before, urged me to interpret the profession of the faith set forth by the holy Fathers assembled at Nicaea, I set myself to this task. He strongly maintained that some villainously pretended both to say and to follow it, but do not any longer have correct thoughts. Rather they distorted what was correctly and consistently said into what seemed good to them.

(5) In order that this might not escape the notice of your holiness, I have sent the book and the document. After you have read it, deign to offer the customary prayers for me.

[2] Cf. Letter 67, note 9.

LETTER 70

Cyril, to the clerics and to Lampon, the priest.[1]

HEN I WAS staying in [the city] of Aelia[2] a certain one of the noble men serving as a soldier in the palace brought to me a large letter of many lines, sealed, saying that he received it from the orthodox in Antioch. The signatures on it were of many clerics, monks and lay persons. They accused the bishops of the East that, although they kept silent about the name of Nestorius, of course, and were pretending to abhor him, they were leaping over to the books of Theodore concerning the Incarnation, in which are lying ready far more dangerous blasphemies than those of Nestorius. He was the father of the evil teaching of Nestorius, and because he voiced the teachings of Nestorius, the impious man is in the company in which he now is. I wrote to the most pious Bishop of Antioch that no one should preach in church the impious teachings of Theodore.

(2) When the most pious deacon and archimandrite, Maximus, arrived in Alexandria, he cried out much against them saying that the orthodox have no place there, nor freedom to speak the dogmas of the true faith. He said that they pretend to confess the creed formulated at Nicaea by the Fathers, but they misinterpret it. He urged me to interpret clearly the entire exposition of the Fathers at Nicaea, in order that they

[1] For the critical text of this letter see Schwartz, *Codex vaticanus gr. 1431*, pp. 16–17. Geerard numbers this letter 5370 in *CPG*.

[2] Aelia Capitolina, the Roman name for Jerusalem. The letter has two parts. The first deals with a letter Cyril received at Jerusalem accusing the bishops of the East of favoring Theodore of Mopsuestia. Cyril comments that he wrote to John of Antioch about this. The second part deals with the arrival of Maximus at Alexandria, evidently from Constantinople. Hence at the end Cyril says "we must fight everywhere" against error.

might not carry off some people by explaining things one way instead of another. I have done this. Accordingly, he is bringing the rolls, so that he may present them to the most pious empresses[3] and to the most Christ-loving and most pious emperor,[4] for I had the book written on parchment. With the help of his consideration, as you[5] may see fit to obtain, may you introduce it at the proper moment.

(3) It is necessary for us to fight everywhere for the true faith and to try as much as is possible to remove from our midst the impiety against Christ which has arisen.

[3] The emperor's wife, Eudoxia, and his sister, Pulcheria.
[4] Theodosius II, emperor from 408 to 450.
[5] Lampon, the priest, was associated with Constantinople. See Letter 3.

LETTER 71

Cyril, to the Emperor Theodosius.[1]

T IS BLAMELESS before God the Father who is in heaven for me to look forward from earth to everlasting life when I say, "Now this alone is everlasting life, that they may know you, the only true God, and him whom you sent, Jesus Christ."[2] But I do not know how some indeed pretend in this regard to walk uprightly, while they are limping and, by deserting the way of truth, turn to another one which leads to extermination and perdition. They cling to the forbidden writing of certain men and, to state the nature of the matter clearly, since it is written, "I spoke of your decrees before kings without being ashamed,"[3] there was a certain Theodore and before him Diodore, the bishop, the latter of Tarsus, the former of Mopsuestia. These were the fathers of the blasphemy of Nestorius. In books which they composed they made use of a crude madness against Christ, the Savior of us all, because they did not understand his mystery. Therefore, Nestorius desired to introduce their teachings into our midst and he was deposed by God.

(2) However, while some bishops of the East anathematized his teachings, in another way they now introduce these very teachings again when they admire the teachings which are Theodore's and say that he thought correctly and in agreement with our Fathers, I mean, Athanasius, Gregory and Basil. But they are lying against holy men. Whatever they wrote, they are the opposite to the wicked opinions of Theo-

[1] For the critical text (only the Latin is extant) on which this letter is based see Schwartz, *ACO* 1.4 pp. 210–211. For another critical text see Schwartz, *ACO* 4.1 p. 108. Geerard numbers this letter 5371 in *CPG*.
[2] Jn 17.3.   [3] Ps 118(119).46.

dore and Nestorius. Therefore, since I have learned that they may bring certain matters concerning these men even to your pious ears, I ask that you preserve your souls entirely intact and clean of the impieties of Theodore and Diodore. As I said above just now, Nestorius stated the teachings which are those of these men, and for this he was condemned as impious by the general council assembled at Ephesus according to the will of God. Since they pretend that they confess the creed which was set forth in the great and ancient synod at Nicaea, but distort its meaning by a false interpretation, the orthodox archimandrites of the East have asked that I explain the meaning of the creed and it has been interpreted.[4]

(3) It was necessary that this work should come to your pious and Christ-loving ears, since among other good things this also is a part of your tranquillity that you choose without ceasing to be delighted by words about the true faith.

[4] In Letter 55.

LETTER 72

Of Cyril, to Proclus, the Bishop of Constantinople, concerning Theodore of Mopsuestia, asking Proclus that he should not permit him to be anathematized since this would be a cause of a disturbance.[1]

ITH DIFFICULTY, at times, and with many labors of your holiness and the holy synod which assembled at Ephesus, the churches of God everywhere rejected the vain babblings of Nestorius. But throughout the East some were exceedingly vexed at this, not only of the laity but also of those assigned to the sacred ministry. Just as the more chronic of illnesses are somehow more difficult regarding medication, or even perhaps entirely reject it, so also a soul sick with the rottenness of distorted thoughts and teachings has an illness hard to cast off. Yet by the grace of God either in pretense or in truth they speak and preach one Christ and anathematize the impious verbiage of Nestorius. In the meanwhile things there are in much tranquillity and they run toward what is steadfast in the faith day by day, even those who once were tottering.

(2) But now, as my lord, the most holy Bishop of Antioch, John, has written to me, the beginning of another storm has arisen among them and quickly there is somehow much alarm lest some of those who are easily carried away would sink down again to what was in the beginning. They say that some arrived at that great city[2] and then approached the most pious and Christ-loving emperors and demanded through their holy sanction that the books of Theodore of Mopsuestia[3] be

---

[1] For the critical text of this letter see Schwartz, *Codex vaticanus gr. 1431*, pp. 17–19. Geerard numbers this letter 5372 in *CPG*.
[2] Constantinople.　　　　　　　[3] Cf. Quasten 3.401–23.

anathematized and the man himself, just named. But his name in the East is great and his writings are admired exceedingly. As they say, all are bearing it hard that a distinguished man, one who died in communion with the churches, now is being anathematized. That we find in his writings some things said strangely and full of unmixed blasphemy is doubtful to no one of those who are accustomed to think the truth.

(3) Let your holiness know that when the exposition composed by him was produced at the holy synod,[4] as those who produced it said, containing nothing healthy, the holy synod condemned it as full of perverted thoughts and, as it were, somehow a spring gushing forth the impiety of Nestorius. But while condemning those who think in this way, in prudence the synod did not mention the man, nor did it subject him to an anathema by name, through prudence, in order that some by paying heed to the opinion of the man might not cast themselves out of the churches. Prudence in these matters is the best thing and a wise one.

(4) If he were still among the living and was a fellow-warrior with the blasphemies of Nestorius, or desired to agree with what he wrote, he would have suffered the anathema also in his own person. But since he has gone to God, it is enough, as I think, that what he wrote absurdly be rejected by those who hold the true doctrines, since by his books being around the chance to go further sometimes begets pretexts for disturbances. And in another way since the blasphemies of Nestorius have been anathematized and rejected, there have been rejected along with them those teachings of Theodore which have the closest connection to those of Nestorius. Therefore, if some of those in the East would do this unhesitatingly, and there was no disturbance expected from it, I would have said that grief at this makes no demands on them now and I would have told them in writing.

(5) But if, as my lord, the most holy Bishop of Antioch, John, writes, they would choose rather to be burned in a fire than do any such thing, for what purpose do we rekindle the

---

[4]The synod at Antioch called by John.

flame that has quieted down and stir up inopportunely the disturbances which have ceased lest perhaps somehow the last may be found to be worse than the first? And I say these things although violently objecting to the things which Theodore, already mentioned, has written and although suspecting the disturbances which will be on the part of some because of the action, lest somehow some may begin to grieve for the teachings of Nestorius as a contrivance in the fashion of that spoken of by the poet among the Greeks,[5] "They mourned in semblance for Patroclus but each one mourned her own sorrows."[6]

(6) If, therefore, these words please your holiness, deign to indicate it, in order that it may be settled by a letter from both of us. It is possible even for those who ask these things to explain the prudence of the matter and persuade them to choose to be quiet rather and not to become an occasion of scandal to the churches.

(7) I have sent to you also the copy of the letter to me from my lord, the most holy bishop, John. When your holiness has read it, you will have a complete insight into the matter.

[5] Homer.
[6] *Il.* 19.302. The women mourn the death of Patroclus. Cyril quotes the entire line.

LETTER 73

Beginning of a letter of Rabbula of blessed memory, written to Saint Cyril, against the impious Theodore.[1]

NOW SOME INDEED in every way reject unity according to subsistence. A hidden disease has become chronic for the East, preying undetected like an incurable wound on the body of the church and though, unnoticed by many, it is secretly honored by supposedly learned men priding [themselves] on their erudition.

(2) A certain bishop, Theodore,[2] of the province of Cilicia, an excellent speaker and powerful persuader, regularly said some things in the pulpit of the church to please the people but fraudulently put in writing other ruinous errors. At the beginning of some of his writings he tried to anathematize the reader not to divulge the writings to others. At first he stated that the Blessed Virgin is not truly the Mother of God, as if the Word of God did not have a birth similar to ours. Lest it be approved by the passing of more time, by God's judgment, Nestorius, unmindful of the new division, published this here-

[1] For the critical text (only the Latin is extant) of this letter see Schwartz, *ACO* 4.1 p. 89. Geerard numbers this letter 5373 in *CPG,* but makes a cross reference to *CPG* 6494. In lines 8–15 of *ACO,* it is stated that Nestorius published Theodore's work as his own. However, Schwartz in *ACO* 1.4 p. 212, lines 23–30 printed an alternate version, which is translated as follows: "A bishop of the province of Cilicia, an excellent speaker and effective persuader, spoke some things from the pulpit to please the people, but in other writings inserted fraudulently erroneous statements. At the beginnings of some of his books he hurled an anathema at the reader not to divulge the writings to others. He was the first to declare that holy Mary is not truly the Mother of God, as if God the Word did not have a human birth as we have. By divine dispensation, lest this [error] hidden till now should be considered truly confirmed by long standing, Nestorius unmindful of [the anathema] has spoken publicly as the author of a new division."

[2] Theodore of Mopsuestia.

tofore latent [error] as its author. This too follows which pertains to the humanity [of Christ]. They do not maintain that
that humanity was joined to the Word of God according to
substance or subsistence, but by some good will, as if the divine nature could not receive another mode of union because
of illimitableness.

(3) He also said that our Lord Jesus Christ must not be
adored as God but because of his relationship he should be
honored as an image of God or rather, to use their terminology, as something resembling an attendant divinity. He
also declared that the Lord's flesh is of no value whatever, dis-
torting the word of the Lord, "the flesh profits nothing."[3] He
says also that the apostles did not know that Christ was God,
and that the church was built on human faith. It is not prudent to put their theorizings about Hell in writing.

(4) These are the collections of their impiety in which they
secretly revelled for a long time and wish, if possible, to cloud
the minds and devout understanding of the people.

[3] Jn 6.64.

LETTER 74

To our holy lord, brother and fellow-servant, bishop Rabbula, Cyril, the bishop, [sends] greetings in our Lord.[1]

ITH INVINCIBLE strength and unshakeable confidence blessed Paul equips our souls when he writes as follows, "Who will separate us from the love of Christ? Tribulation, or distress, or persecution, or hunger, or nakedness, or danger, or the sword?"[2] For nothing is intolerable to those who hold themselves resolved to fight the good fight of faith, to finish the course, to keep the faith, so as to reach the immortal crown.[3] For just as those who understand how to steer a ship properly, not just when they travel in peaceful weather but when they save their ship from stormy waves, will be known as skilled helmsmen, so also they to whom the guidance of the holy churches is entrusted shine forth, not in peaceful stability of affairs, but their wisdom manifests itself more widely in trials, in endurance and fortitude, and in their robust resistance against the shameful inventions which the heretics invent from their hearts.

(2) Consequently your holiness, my lord, has always indeed shone round about, but most especially now when you have become the pillar and base of the truth[4] for all the inhabitants

---

[1] The text of the letter is preserved in Syriac. It was published by J. J. Overbeck, *S. Ephraemi Syri, Rabbulae episc. Edesseni, Balaei aliorumque opera selecta* (Oxford, 1865), 226–229. It was translated into German by Gustav Bickell, *Ausgewählte Schriften der syrischen Kirchenväter Aphraates, Rabulas und Isaak von Ninive* (Kempten: Kösel, 1874), 246–249. The German translation is here rendered by me into English. Schwartz, in *ACO* 4.1 p. 87, published the first part in Latin, and my English rendering is appended as an alternate version. Geerard numbers this letter 5374 in *CPG*.

[2] Cf. Rom 8.35.   [3] Cf. 2 Tm 4. 7, 8.

[4] Cf. 1 Tm 3.15.

of the East, and are driving out like a deadly disease the abominable and newly sprouted blasphemies of Nestorius which are derived from another root, I mean, Theodore of Cilicia.[5] For from there this ungodliness took its beginning. But that one[6] hoped that he would stretch over the whole world his dominion that originated from the power which had been given him, I do not know how. For he usurped unto himself the exalted throne and became the prey of the many-headed dragon,[7] but he hoped to swallow up the Church of God and to subjugate all to himself.

(3) Yea, if almighty God had not saved us, then perhaps his wish might have gone to fulfillment, as that godless one had hoped that the church would fall into his hands, in accordance with the zeal of his accomplices.[8] But, on the contrary, it was as the prophet says, "Our God is with us. Know this, you pagans, and be overcome, you strong ones! For if to you yourselves you appear ever so strong, yet you will be still overcome. Every plan which you concocted, the Lord will bring to naught and no assault which you mount will have permanence; for the Lord, our God, is with us."[9]

(4) Therefore, God protects the herald of his truth, but he vehemently shakes and annihilates the power of his enemies, and brings their designs to naught, so that they do not attain to the goal of their expectation.

(5) Your perfection should not let itself be disturbed by the threats of those who according to their custom wantonly and imprudently threaten everyone, since they make themselves into servants of the blasphemies of Nestorius. These people have absolutely no episcopal authority whatever, because the holy synod[10] has defined all that as void which they could venture to undertake against anyone. But all the holy bishops who dwell within the confines of the Romans are one and all joined with your glorious holiness in intention, will, zeal, agreement, communion and belief. For you shine forth so

---

[5] Theodore of Mopsuestia.
[7] Cf. Rv 13.1–10.
[9] Cf. Is 8.8–10.

[6] Nestorius.
[8] The Latin text in Schwartz ends here.
[10] Council of Ephesus. See Letter 27.

much, you strengthen in the truth through your wise advice
as well those who are under your guidance as also the inhabitants in other cities and lands and admonish not only those
adjacent to your holiness but also those far off.

(6) But as to the censure of the godless, as to their abuse
and former hatefulness of that kind, it is of little consequence
to me. For if they named our Lord, Beelzebub,[11] then it is also
nothing new if they name me thus. And if they have per-
secuted him, how should they not also persecute me? But in
all these things we prevail and our labor brings it about that
the harvest, the love of Christ, increases and we reach the im-
perishable glory. For that your wise perfection in all things
is in good stead to lead the regions adjacent to you along
the right path and to teach the word of faith clearly and dis-
tinctly.

(7) But on account of the people who go astray and praise
the heresy which was introduced in our time through Nestorius in order to seize and lead astray the foolish, I necessarily
also in proportion to my ability have placed this treatise in opposition to his false teaching, as was my duty, and have written
it in a book in which I refute his blasphemies through the
power of truth. I have sent this also to your holiness[12] and
thereby you might show me the kindness and courtesy to im-
prove in it what exceeds my mental capacity and also, if this
seems good and advantageous to you, to permit it to be read
before the faithful brethren. I have, moreover, in addition
written a treatise about the Incarnation of the Son of God[13]
for the faithful emperor, which I enclose for your holiness,
and, if it seems proper to you that this also be read before the
faithful brethren, do so, whatever appears good to you. For I
also have read the letters sent to me by your perfection before
all the clergy and before all the bishops who assemble with me
in Alexandria, while I pointed out to them thereby that Christ

[11] Cf. Mt 10.25 and Mk 3.22.
[12] Cyril is referring to his work, *Against the Blasphemies of Nestorius*, composed in 430. See Quasten 3.126. See also Letters 34 and 44.
[13] See Quasten 3.126–127 and Letter 43.

is not sleeping[14] but has lights in all places which fill all the places of life.

(8) But when your perfection has read the contents in the books then you will scorn such people who revile me as if I had maintained that the divine nature would be capable of suffering, or as if I had followed the opinion of Apollinaris or any other false teaching. For if your holiness pays attention to these writings carefully, you will perceive that in the entire book the contents of the chapter[15] laid down by me earlier will be exactly carried out whereby also thus the shafts discharged from the widely gaping mouth of the adversaries against me would be made harmless. This will be enough for your piety.

[14] Cf. Mt 8.25, Mk 4.38 and Lk 8.23.

[15] The twelve anathemas against Nestorius at the end of Letter 17 to which the Eastern bishops took offense.

LETTER 74
(Alternate Version)

Cyril, to Rabbula of Edessa.[1]

O A CERTAIN incomparable eagerness and to unshake-able confidence the very wise Paul arouses our souls writing as follows, "Who shall separate us from the love of Christ? Shall tribulation, or distress, or persecution, or hunger, or nakedness, or danger, or the sword?"[2] For nothing is intolerable to those who hold themselves resolved to fight the fight of faith, to finish the course, to keep the faith, so that they may deserve the crown of immortality.[3]

(2) But just as being able to save a ship in a storm, not just to sail one in a calm, shows they are the most approved who are accustomed to steer best, so also complete calmness of affairs does not show that those assigned to preside over the churches are renowned, but skill in tribulations, and bravery, and patience, and strongly resisting the unstable words of heretics. Your holiness has always indeed been splendid but especially now since you have become the pillar and foundation of the truth[4] to all in the East, and, as it were, are driving out a certain pestilential disease, the blasphemy of the new and abominable heresy of Nestorius.

(3) For that impiety is indeed proceeding from another root, I mean, his who was of Cilicia,[5] and he[6] thought that he would take hold of the whole world because of a power given to him, though I do not know how. He seized a most powerful

---

[1] For the critical text (only the Latin is extant) of this letter see Schwartz, *ACO* 4.1 p. 87.

[2] Rom 8.35.

[3] Cf. 2 Tm 4. 7, 8.

[4] Cf. 1 Tm 3.15.

[5] Theodore of Mopsuestia.

[6] Nestorius.

seat and has become prey for the dragon having many heads,[7] but he[8] hoped also to swallow up the holy churches of God and to seize all, and unless almighty God had saved us he certainly would have prevailed insofar as pertains to the power of his attempts and the accursed attacks of those who are near to him.

[7] Cf. Rv 13.1–10.   [8] Nestorius.

LETTER 75

The letter of blessed Atticus, Bishop of Constantinople, to the most blessed Cyril, Archbishop of Alexandria, containing the request suggested, as if by the decision of the emperor, that the title of John was written in the diptychs.[1]

E HAVE FALLEN into what we did not deliberately choose and we are forced to agree with what has happened to us, not according to our opinion, because we preferred what was advantageous to what was just, and were inclined in our reasonings toward the harmony of the people, and not because we were mutilating the canons of the Fathers, but because we placed the peace of the world before precise subtlety of words. So I know that the blessed Paul in legislating for the churches wisely administered the affairs. I know also that your father among the saints, Theophilus,[2] equal to the apostles, in the Greek disturbance honored peace before precision for a short time. The greatest of the cities, like unto the billows of the billowing sea, has come to be controlled according to the opinions of the inhabitants and not so much by laws and precise arrangement, as by easily mastered judgments looking toward peace and concord.

(2) But learn for what reason I send these letters. Your holiness somehow thoroughly knew, or rather has been seen by those eyes with which our saintly father, the most God-loving

---

[1] For the critical text of this letter see Schwartz, *Codex vaticanus gr. 1431*, pp. 23–24. Geerard numbers this letter 5375 in *CPG*. This letter and the next are out of place in time in the collection. The date is about 412–415.

[2] Theophilus, Patriarch at Alexandria 385–412, the uncle and predecessor of Cyril, in the Synod of the Oak in 403 had deposed St. John Chrysostom from his see in Constantinople. Arsacius, John's successor, died in 405, John died in 407, and Atticus, now Bishop of Constantinople, returned to communion with Rome by restoring John's title to the diptychs, the list of the living and the dead to be commemorated at the Eucharist.

Theophilus,[3] saw, what kind and how great a disorder seized
the capital city and that the pious faith was in danger of being
shaken apart from the depths. The people, split for the most
part, gathered outside the walls and the priests and our fellow
bishops were torn apart from communion with each other almost ripping apart the good planting of Christ our Lord, I
mean, the beauty of peace. With much toil and with dangers
full of disappointment the greater part and the most important of them were put to rest by the prayers and sighs of our
common Fathers and also by those of your holiness. And concord and tranquillity possess the churches throughout the
world.

(3) Afterwards some desired that the title alone of blessed
John[4] be written on the sacred diptychs,[5] so that even the
blessed bishop Alexander, I mean the Bishop of Antioch,
having stopped at the capital city[6] spoke many bold words,
and wished very much to stir up the people, so that, even
though we did not wish it, he would force the title just mentioned to be inscribed. These actions the servants of God, the
most pious deacons, Peter and Aedesius, have explained with
all accuracy in every way no doubt to your holiness.

(4) But after much time went by and we were constraining
the pressure from the populace, and were in no way going
back to the remnant of the schism,[7] the most God-loving
bishop, Acacius, wrote to us from the East that Theodotus,
the most pious Bishop of Antioch had been forced by the
people to inscribe the title of John, and he asked that we grant
him pardon because he had done this through necessity. When
that noble presbyter, the one who delivered the letter, first
scattered the purpose for which he came among the people of
the capital city, and passed on to the people the purport of the
letter to us, so that the crowd almost filled every place to over-
flowing, then indeed, I made a plea concerning the peace of
the capital city and a tranquil state of affairs, because I was

[3] There is a play on words in the Greek: *theophilestatos/Theophilos.*
[4] John Chrysostom.　　　　　　　[5] The diptychs.
[6] Constantinople.
[7] Atticus was not in communion with Rome until he restored John's title to
the diptychs.

disturbed and feared a crisis in the most important matters, and since I was in the presence of the most pious emperor.[8] But the most pious emperor answered that there was no harm in inscribing the title of a dead man for the sake of tranquillity, and the harmony and peace of the populace.

(5) Accordingly, persuaded by these words, I prepared the title to be inscribed. For how was I to anticipate the necessity that matters with us might not become an obedience to the crowd, and that the city might not be placed under the rule of the mob? In no way, as I think, have I wronged the canons themselves, nor have I disgraced the judgment of the Fathers. He is commemorated not only with the bishops who have died, but also with the presbyters, deacons, and laymen and women with all of whom there is not a sharing with us of the priesthood nor a participation in what is mystically performed at the holy table. There is a great difference between those who have gone past the goal and those still existing on earth, so that even the lists are separated according to the state of those mentioned. Neither did the honorable burial of Saul injure David in any way, nor did Eudoxius the follower of the impiety of Arius injure the apostles although he is lying beneath the same altar, nor did Paulinus and Evagrius,[9] who were leaders of the schism of the Church of Antioch, who, after death, not many years ago, were inscribed in the spiritual diptychs to bring about the peace and harmony of the people.

(6) Hence, do you yourself, most God-loving lord, command that the title of him who has died be inscribed in the churches throughout Egypt for the sake of universal peace. In this you are not transgressing the canons of the Fathers, but you are making of the greatest worth the simultaneous harmony of all the churches.

(7) I have been fully assured that you will write to us what is fitting, since you look to the common unanimity of the brotherhood. I and all who are with me greet the brotherhood with you. Farewell.

[8] Theodosius II, emperor 408–450.
[9] Cf. Quasten 3.40, 206–207.

LETTER 76

[Letter] of holy Cyril, Bishop of Alexandria, to the most holy Atticus, Bishop of Constantinople concerning the same title of John, Bishop of Constantinople.[1]

HAVING READ WHAT was sent by your holiness[2] I learned that the title of John had been inscribed on the sacred tablets. But, having asked those who came from there, I learned that his title was placed, not in the lists of the laity, but in the lists of the bishops. Considering and thinking within myself whether those who have done this are following the decrees of the Fathers at Nicaea, and scarcely turning the eye of my mind toward that great synod, I see the entire assembly of those holy Fathers as if in some way disagreeing with their eyes and with all their strength stopping us from running toward agreement in this matter.

(2) How will he who was cast out from episcopal functions be placed with the bishops of God and bear their lot? How will he who was placed outside ecclesiastical walls be in the lists of sacred ministers? For we must either say that the name of the episcopacy is nothing and that that, which is a matter reserved only to those called to it, is common to all, or, if it is something great which divides the episcopacy and the laity, do not mingle what cannot be mingled, but keep each of those mentioned in their proper rank and deem each worthy of the honor proper to him.

(3) How, therefore, will you indicate the people among the

---

[1] For the critical text of this letter see Schwartz, *Codex vaticanus gr. 1431*, pp. 25–28. Geerard numbers this letter 5376 in *CPG*. This letter is out of place in the collection. It dates from an early period in Cyril's life, about 415.

[2] In this reply Cyril objects to John Chrysostom's title being listed. In 417 he was persuaded by Isidore of Pelusium to agree.

bishops, or one, who is not a noble, among the nobles? Honor, I bid you, those who have given witness by great and brilliant actions. Do not insult the holy assembly of the Fathers. Consider those who are still present and alive with us. How would they be disposed to what has happened? Would they not rightly say that they have been filled with much grief, if he who was deposed is introduced to the same rank as they? I think that your holiness also is persuaded of this.

(4) Therefore, remove for them and for us the pretext of disgust. Take away the basis of the sorrow of all. To arrange manageably what occurs unexpectedly I would say is good and wise, but it will be wise, then, if it introduces no injury. And we do not increase the fold of Christ by taking in swarms of those in heresy, even if they do not change their wandering from the fold. For this reason it is absolutely necessary to greet some accommodating and poorly worked out peace with those against whom battle is greater.

(5) Actually, it is the task of prudence to appear sometimes to depart somewhat from the proper position with foregoing of loss in useful circumstances. So also the blessed Paul "became all things to all men",[3] not in order that he might gain some short advantage, but that, with the loss of a part, he might gain all.

(6) Let us see, therefore, as we go on in the investigation in these matters, whether the postulate that these actions seem to be good does not contain the greater harm. So much time has passed by since your holiness took the throne, and yet there is no one declining to be reconciled. Even if some at the beginning acted rather contentiously and kept themselves away, these also have been called back through the strength and grace of our Savior. Which of those in authority is there who does not heed your reverence? Who is there who has remained outside the church because of this?[4] There is no one. May God grant that there may be no one. Therefore, to save whom or to call whom to a reconciliation, do you place outside

[3] 1 Cor. 9.22.
[4] John's title not being in the diptychs.

the walls of the church Egypt and the cohort under the prefect of Egypt, Arcadia, the Thebaid, Libya, and Pentapolis,
and cause grief to so many churches? In order to gain no one.
The grace of the Savior has gained them already. I refer your
labor in this matter to the teachings of your holiness. Do not,
therefore, accuse yourself for those who are of a contentious
opinion and who do not ever accept a just decision on this
subject.

(7) Has your holiness assumed that we are napping to such
a degree that we would not diligently try to inquire about your
reputation, and how the flocks of the Savior are being led?
The concern of bishops is the same even though we are separated by place. In order that I may not seem to exert myself
excessively in this matter and think the opposite to your holiness, granted that there are some few totally at variance still
being endangered because of his[5] dishonor, yet with us there
are so many churches strongly maintaining that the decrees
against him are in force. For whom, therefore, is it just to
enjoy a vote? To accommodate whom is it more pleasing to
God? [Is it more pleasing to God to accommodate] those who
pleaded the causes of him who suffered such outrages as those
who determined to censure him, whereby to grieve the Savior
is reckoned as nothing? If, therefore, saving the unanimity of
the churches does not appear contemptible, undo that which
severs it, I beg you. "Put your sword into its scabbard."[6] Order
the title of John to be removed from the list of bishops.

(8) If we calculate that this is nothing, let a listing of the be-
trayer with them not vex the assembly of the apostles, but,
when the name of Judas is introduced, where thereafter will
Matthias be placed by us? If, therefore, no one, by throwing
Matthias out, would inscribe Judas in the assembly of the
apostles, let there remain and be preserved, I urge you, after
Nectarius of famed memory, in the next place the all-glorious
Arsacius, lest something introduced by force might drive out
the memory of the blessed man. Perhaps a few are vexed
greatly by this. Permit me to speak with freedom. We pray

[5] John Chrysostom.   [6] Jn 18.11.

that all be saved. If anyone out of his own ignorance is separated and resists the precepts of the church, what is the loss of
this man? Did not the Savior himself, when teaching us this
very thing and setting an example in all things, say what was
good for those who came to him and permit those to go away
who refused and would not agree? So far had he stood aloof
from having a discussion with such men that he even said to
his disciples, "Do you also wish to go away?"[7] It is just for us to
apportion a great deal of care on those who accept him.

(9) The disaffected and disobedient man would blame his
own malice because he hated the cure. He will hear from the
just judge, "When I spoke, you did not even obey, and I pro-
longed my words to you and you did not heed,"[8] and the
words following. But for us who teach those things for which
one might be held in esteem by God, it is proper to give instructions very zealously and to say with Paul to those who refuse, "We exhort you, for Christ's sake, be reconciled to God,"[9]
and to entrust the disobedient to the power of God, saying,
"We would have healed Babylon, but she was not healed. We
left her, for her judgment reached up to heaven."[10] It is, therefore, not consistent, because of the opposition of some men, if
indeed there are any at all, to shake to their foundations, as it
were, the ordinances of the church by assigning laity to the
position of those distinguished in the episcopacy, and placing
them in an equal measure of honor. Let not some call this a
universal peace but rather a mutilation. I say that then the
name and reality of peace is supreme when we do not set ourselves against the opinions of the saints and do not act against
their decrees. Even if the blessed Alexander, being really
overconfident of speech according to the expression of your
holiness, has imposed upon and swept along and carried
some of our most pious brothers and fellow bishops in the
East to an agreement in this matter, the sickness ought not for
this reason utterly to hold sway and feed upon the souls of all.
Like a soreness infecting the eye of the church, it ought to be

[7] Jn 6.68.
[8] Cf. Is 65.12.
[9] 2 Cor 5.20.
[10] Cf. Jer 28.9.

cleansed by you, so that, since it again looks to the decrees of the Fathers, rightly it may hear from Christ, "Your eyes are doves." [11]

(10) Therefore, I also have received a letter from the most God-loving bishop, Acacius, a man most happy in his old age, in which he strongly maintains that the most pious Bishop of Antioch was forced by some to celebrate the memory of John, and that he was deeply stung by this. He was seeking to find some escape from recklessness and desiring to receive a letter concerning this from us and from your holiness clearly saying that he should not be led astray with some persons nor submit to those advising such actions. Let us, who have been called to serve others (permit me to speak with freedom since I am distressed in my soul), not become an increase of wounds, in order that we may avoid being an accompaniment of the recklessness of others. I wonder at this, namely, if the bishop mentioned before, Alexander, being a man with such a flow of words, and having spent no small time there, not only appears by his power to have persuaded some men of this, but a single person, the deliverer of the letter, was so strong, as it has been rumored, that he inflamed the people so much and again stirred up a cause which had been put to rest a long time ago. This is entirely unbelievable. Let it stand, and let it be believed that this happened, yet I know that your reverence is outstanding in words. You will in every way teach those who have been disturbed what they ought to learn. You have the sufficient grace of your holy preaching. I know that you will also persuade the most reverent emperors to agree in their usual way to the decree in the canons. Being pious and Christ-loving they will permit the churches to be administered and being zealous of their ancestral virtue they will imitate their example. Therefore, let Jeconiah,[12] who was cast out, not be set in equal place with David and Samuel, the prophets.

(11) If it seemed good, incorrectly, to some to put the corpse of Eudoxius in the place you mentioned, do we because of this consider the unholy as holy? It was doubtless necessary that a

[11] Song 1.15.   [12] Cf. Est 2.6.

correction in this matter be sought by us rather, and not that
he conform to what was after him. We say this, not as men
who trample upon one fallen, God forbid, nor rejoicing in the
evils of others, as it is written,[13] for this is not the intention of
Christians, but because of sympathy toward the man we are
doing what is beneficial to the church and consider nothing
more honorable than her canons. If it was possible that nothing in them be violated, and that the one deposed be classed
among the bishops, rightly those who hinder this being done
would be called fierce and savage. Since it is necessary that,
when one man is ruling, the power of another be taken away,
let the ordinances of the church prevail. Let him who is not a
bishop be removed from the clerical lists. This unites the
churches unto peace. May this accomplish for us complete
harmony.

(12) Grant, therefore, to us that we may be united perfectly
with your holiness since you make your love toward those still
living, or rather the ordinances of the church, more important than the love of one man who is even dead.

[13] Cf. Prov 17.5 and 2 Cor 10.15.

LETTER 77

Cyril, to my lord, my beloved brother and fellow bishop, Domnus, greetings in the Lord. A copy of a synodical letter.[1]

IT IS NECESSARY for us[2] to grieve with our brothers, especially those of our fellow bishops who maintain that they have suffered in some way, and this at the hands of their own clerics who necessarily should bend their necks as to a father and be subject according to what seems best to God and is fully related in the canons of the church. How is such daring not one of the most disgraceful things?

(2) The most pious bishop Athanasius says that he has suffered such treatment and he gave the tearful message that he was driven out, when the synod assembled in the royal city of Constantinople. For he says that some of those who were themselves clerics seized power to such an extent that, insofar as the force of their undertakings went, they expelled him from the episcopacy and brought forth a vote of deposition against him. For they desire to cast out the administrators of the church, or certainly the managers of ecclesiastical affairs, and put in place by themselves those who are of their own opinion.

(3) In addition to these actions he says that they remove his name from the sacred diptychs, and do some other things discordant and full of impiety, which the meaning of the petitions attached encompasses. It is absurd that such things be

---

[1] For the critical text of this letter see Schwartz, *ACO* 2.1.3 pp. 66 (425), 67 (426). Geerard numbers this letter 5377 in *CPG*.

[2] Domnus, Archbishop of Antioch, successor to John of Antioch. This letter, unlike the previous two, deals with matters of Cyril's later life. An attempt to depose Athanasius was made by his clerics.

dared on the part of clerics against their own bishops and it is
impossible to overlook these matters.

(4) Let your holiness deign, if the city of Antioch is far from
that which the most God-fearing bishop, Athanasius, mentioned previously, was assigned to administer, to grant a hearing to certain people through a letter of your own. Then
those who are bearing the accusation may answer when addressed, and if they should be found liable to the accusations,
they may be kept away from the sacred ministry. What they
themselves have ventured to do against their own father, this
they should justly suffer, since they have paid no heed to any
conformity, have gone beyond every ordinance, and deemed
it nothing to dishonor a father's dignity.

(5) Besides, it is said that they have not now for the first time
begun to act so, but already have been condemned in many
worse and brazen undertakings. He[3] says that he considers
suspect the one assigned to the metropolitan jurisdiction of
the territory from which he is, and, as I said already, there is
no grief that those in suspicion are not able to judge him.

(6) Greet the brotherhood with you. Those with me greet
you in the Lord.

[3] Athanasius.

LETTER 78

Cyril, to Domnus.[1]

ACH OF OUR AFFAIRS, when it proceeds rightly in canonical good order, begets in us no disturbance, and
even releases us from obloquy on the part of some, or
rather it gains good repute for us from those who think properly. Who would not accept an unbiased vote, that is to say,
one which is cast by some. How will judging rightly and according to the law not be unblameworthy, but rather full of all
praise?

(2) I write these words now to your holiness because in the
letters sent to me and to our most holy and most God-fearing
brother and fellow bishop, Proclus,[2] your holiness named the
most pious and God-loving bishop, Peter, and said that he was
lamenting and saying that he had been removed unexpectedly from the church assigned to him. The consequence was
that either he had the name of the episcopacy along with the
actuality, or he did not deserve to preside at the holy altar,
and be honored by the very title of bishop. Perhaps our statement would seem to your reverence to be harsh and somewhat lacking in mutual love. In truth it is not so.

(3) Indeed we think that the old man is to be pitied, if we
take away only the title, but it was much better to consider another matter also. He says that he is not able to struggle with
the prejudice against him, and he did not get a chance of
a defense, nor was a canonical hearing granted to him. But

---

[1] For the critical text of this letter see Joannou, *Fonti,* 2.276–281. Geerard
numbers this letter 5378 in *CPG*.

[2] Archbishop of Constantinople, cf. Letter 72.

94

if some such a thing had happened, the very collection of
the records would have proved him either convicted by the
charges, or would have revealed him liable and having nothing left to say about injustice done him. On the other hand, it
would have revealed him free of the charges and would have
given back again the authority over the church which was
under his jurisdiction. Since nothing like this has been done,
he cries out against the act and says he has undergone unbearable injustice and has been ejected illegally, charging in
addition that all the money he had at hand was snatched away
from him.

(4) May your holiness, therefore, considering what is decreed in the holy canons and what is proper for the church
and for those assigned to the sacred ministry and, in addition
to this, being troubled at this letter from us, cause the weeping of the old man to cease. And if he should choose to be
judged before those bringing charges against him, let him be
tried according to custom before your holiness and, of course,
all the most God-fearing bishops under his jurisdiction, unless he might decline some as suspect. We believe that none of
the most God-fearing bishops has hostile thoughts about a
brother. In order that this may not become a pretext dissolv-
ing the judgment which is about to come into being concerning him in consequence of it not appearing to have been made
in justice, there is no dismay in some of those under suspicion
being away from the synod.

(5) With regard to the money taken from him unjustly, it is
right that it be given back according to two ways of reasoning.
First, that it was not necessary at all that such a thing happen,
and secondly, that it is extremely distressing and weighs down
to the ultimate of exhaustion the most God-fearing bishops
who are throughout the world, that accounts of the management of the expenditures which befall them are required
whether from ecclesiastical income or from the revenue of
other sources. Each of us will give an account of our own
wrongdoings to the judge of all. It is necessary that the treasures and the immovable possessions of the church be pre-

served, and it is necessary that the management of the expenditures which occur in the timely administration of the sacred ministry be confidently credited.

(6) He says that the documents of abdication were extracted from him not by his own choice but as from necessity, fear, and the threatening of some people. That is a different matter, nor is it agreeable to the ordinances of the church to force any persons in the sacred ministry to accept the documents of abdication. If they are worthy of the sacred ministry, let them remain in it. If they are unworthy, let them not leave it by an abdication, but rather be sentenced for their deeds, about which matters someone might make a great outcry to the effect that they stray beyond all conformity.

(7) Greet the brothers with you; those with us salute you in the Lord.

LETTER 79

Cyril, to the bishops who are in Libya and Pentapolis.[1]

T IS NECESSARY to take thought about completing every useful and necessary thing for the edification of the people and for the good reputation of the churches, for it is written, "Make holy the sons of Israel."[2] Accordingly, the fathers of the monasteries in the province of Thebes, pious men who have a not unadmired administration, coming to Alexandria, and being asked by me about the condition of the monasteries there, explained that many are scandalized because of this reason.

(2) Some men, recently married, and almost having just come from the very bridal chambers, are seizing some of the most God-loving bishops and, doubtless, with no one reporting the facts concerning them, are being ordained clerics, that is, priests. Some others, after being thrown out of the monasteries as undisciplined, are also stealthily gaining ordinations and, becoming clerics, are entering even into the very monasteries from which they were expelled, and desire to offer sacrifice and perform those functions which it is customary for clerics to fulfill. Some of those who know them refuse to attend their religious services and refuse to tolerate any share in their liturgies.

(3) Since, therefore, as I said, all things must be done on our part toward the edification of the people, let your reverence look to these matters and, if anyone is about to be ordained a cleric, let your reverence thoroughly investigate his

[1] For the critical text of this letter see Joannou, *Fonti*, 2.281–284. Geerard numbers this letter 5379 in *CPG*.
[2] Cf. Lev 15.31.

97

life, both as to whether he has a wife or not, and how and when he married her, and if he is not one of those expelled either by another God-fearing bishop, or from a monastery, then let him be ordained after he has been found blameless. Thus we will preserve both our own conscience clean and the holy and august ministry blameless.

(4) If some are subject to an excommunication, since they have been punished because of lapses and then are about to die while they are catechumens, let them be baptized and do not let them depart from among men having no share of grace, that is, excommunicated. This, too, seems to be in conformity with the ordinances of the church.

(5) Greet the brothers with you; those with me salute you in the Lord.

LETTER 80

To Optimus, the bishop.[1]

. . . and at all events seeing with pleasure your virtuous disciples both because of their stability beyond their years and on account of their innate reverence for you, from which it is possible to expect some great advantage for them.[2] When I saw them coming to me with your letter, affection for them doubled. When I read your letter and saw in it both the foresight of your care concerning the churches and also attention in the reading of the Holy Scriptures, I gave thanks to the Lord. I prayed for good things for those who have brought such a letter to us and, even before them, for the one who wrote to us.

(2) You asked about that well-known saying which has been turned around, up and down by everyone, as to what the saying has for a solution, "Whoever kills Cain shall be punished sevenfold."[3] Because of this, to begin with, you are carefully guarding the advice to Timothy which Paul gave, for you obviously are "diligent in reading."[4] Then, too, you have restored us, an old man who has grown stiff with age and weakness of body and a multitude of afflictions, for the number of them stirred up in us has oppressed our life,[5] and, by warm-

---

[1] This letter is not by Cyril. It was written by Basil the Great probably in 377. For the Greek text see PG 77.365–72. Geerard numbers this letter 5380 in *CPG*. For another English translation see A. C. Way, trans., *Saint Basil: Letters Volume 2 (186–368)*, FOTC 28 (Washington, D.C.: The Catholic University of America Press, 1955), 222–32. For Optimus, see E. Venables, "Optimus (1)" in *A Dictionary of Christian Biography, Literature, Sects and Doctrines During the First Eight Centuries*, eds. William Smith and Henry Wace, 4 vols. (London, 1877–87), 4:95.
[2] The letter begins with an incomplete sentence.
[3] Gn 4.15. [4] Cf. 1 Tm 4.13.
[5] These words refer to Basil's age and health, not to Cyril's.

ing us who have been refreshed by your spirit, you have aroused what lay torpid as in a den of beasts unto reasonable wakefulness and vital energy.

(3) Therefore it is possible that the saying be understood simply and show an unadorned meaning. Hence the more simple explanation which all can defend handily is this, that it is necessary for Cain to pay the penalty seven times over for the crimes he committed. It is not the part of a just judge to determine retributions equal for equal, but it is necessary that the perpetrator of evil repay what is due with interest, or intend to become better because of the punishments and make others be more self-restrained by his example.

(4) Therefore, since it has been decreed that Cain satisfy justice seven times for his crimes, it says that the one who killed him will pay the penalty in equal measure to that decreed against Cain by the divine judgment. This is the meaning following upon the first reading of it. Since the mind has been made to examine the depths of troublesome things, it asks justice how he fulfills what is due in the sevenfold punishment, whether there are seven sins, or, on the one hand, one sin, but, on the other hand, seven punishments for the one.

(5) Scripture always defines the number of the forgiveness for sins in sevens. "How often shall my brother sin against me, and I forgive him?" Peter is speaking to the Lord. "Up to seven times?" Then the answer of the Lord, "I do not say to you seven times, but seventy times seven,"[6] for the Lord did not pass on to another number, but by multiplying seven placed the limit at it. After seven years the Hebrew was released from slavery. Seven weeks of years made the glorious jubilee for those of old in which the earth kept a sabbath, a cancellation of debts was necessary, release from bondage, and, as it were, a new life from the very start was ordained through the number seven since the old one in some manner received its completion.[7] But these were figures of this age which, revolving through seven days, hastens by us, in which

6 Mt 18.21, 22.   7 Cf. Lv 25.1–12.

payments in full are made for our more moderate[8] sins according to the benevolent care of the good Lord, lest we be given over unto punishment in the age which is endless. Therefore the sevenfold is used because of its relation toward this world, so that since men love this world, they may be punished for what they owe, because of which they chose to do wrong. If you count up for someone the crimes committed by Cain you will find seven, and if you arrange what was decided by the judge against him, you will not thus miss the sense.

(6) Therefore, the first sin of those which Cain dared to commit was envy for the preference for Abel.[9] The second was the deceit with which he spoke to his brother, saying, "Let us go out into the field."[10] The third was murder. The fourth was an addition of evil, because the murder of a brother is a greater intensity of evil. The fifth was that Cain, the first murderer, was leaving behind a bad example for posterity. The sixth wrongdoing was that he caused grief to his parents. The seventh was that he lied to God, for when asked, "Where is your brother Abel, he answered, 'I do not know.'"[11] He, the Lord, unleashed seven penalties on the murder of Cain.[12]

(7) When the Lord said, "Cursed are you in the soil which has opened its mouth to receive your brother's blood, and groaning and trembling shall you be on the earth, Cain said, 'If you drive me today from the soil, from your face I shall be hidden. And I shall be groaning and trembling on the earth, and whoever finds me will kill me.' In reply to this the Lord said, 'Not so! Whoever kills Cain shall be punished sevenfold.'"[13] Since Cain thought that he was easy to be caught by anyone, because he did not have security on earth, for the earth was accursed because of him, and he had been stripped of the help of God, who was angered at him because of the murder, since there was support left for him, neither from

---

[8] More moderate than Cain's crime. Basil is speaking of the week of seven days.
[9] Cf. Gn 4.5–7.   [10] Gn 4.8.
[11] Gn 4.9.   [12] Cf. Gn 4.15.
[13] Cf. Gn 4.10–15. "Groaning and trembling" is the sense Basil takes from the words as is seen later in the letter.

earth nor from heaven, he says, "It will be that everyone finding me will kill me." [14] The answer corrects his mistake saying,
"Not so," that is, you will not be killed. [15] But Cain not only
conceals his festering sore, but also adds a lie to the murder
by joining to it, "I do not know. Am I my brother's keeper?" [16]

(8) From here on the Lord begins to count the punishments. "Cursed are you in the soil." [17] This is the first punishment. "Till the soil." [18] This is the second one. A certain un-
speakable necessity was imposed upon him, impelling him
toward the work of the land, so that it was not possible for
him, even if he desired it, to cease, but always it forced him to
be wearied out by the soil being hostile to him, which he had
made accursed by having polluted it with the blood of a
brother. A life with those who hate you is a terrible punishment, to have an enemy as a fellow inhabitant, and to have a
hatred unceasing. "Till the soil" that is, exerting yourself in
the works of agriculture you will slacken at no time, being set
free of the labors, neither by night nor by day, having necessity rousing you up to the tasks harsher than any master and
you will not add to its power to give you food.

(9) Yet even if the unceasing kind of laboring has some
fruit, the very labor itself is not a moderate torment for the
one always striving and working hard. Both the labor is unceasing, and the hardship concerning the soil is fruitless, that
is, the fruitlessness of the labors. [19] "Groaning and trembling
shall you be on the earth." [20] He imposed two other punishments to the other three, namely, uninterrupted groaning
and trembling of the body, since his limbs do not have support
from his bodily strength. Since he made evil use of the strength
of his body, the tone of his muscles was taken away from him.
He is agitated and shaken, and is able neither to bring food
easily to his mouth nor to carry a drink, since his evil hand

[14] Gn 4.14.
[15] Gn 4.15. A long passage of Basil's letter is omitted here.
[16] Gn 4.9.   [17] Gn 4.11
[18] Gn 4.12.   [19] This is the third punishment.
[20] Cf. Gn 4.12.

with its unholy deed is not able any longer to assist to the utmost the personal and necessary needs of the body.

(10) Another punishment is that which Cain revealed by saying, "If you drive me now from the soil, from your face I shall be hidden."[21] The heaviest punishment for those of sound mind is separation from God. It will come about, he says, that, "whoever finds me will kill me." He is conjecturing from the consequence of what went before. If you have driven me from the soil, if I shall be hidden from your face, there remains that I be killed by anyone. What then does the Lord say? "Not so."[22] He put a mark upon him; this is the seventh punishment. The fact that he could not hide the punishment but that it was heralded before him by a clearly seen sign that this is the doer of the impious deeds, for those who read it rightly, is the harshest disgrace of the punishments, which we also have learned about the last judgment when some will rise up unto everlasting life and others unto everlasting shame and reproach.[23]

(11) A kindred question follows this, namely, the statement made by Lamech to his wives, "I kill a man for wounding me, and a youth for bruising me."[24] The wound is one thing and the bruise another; and the man is one person and the youth another. Since because of Cain sevenfold punishment was decreed, because of Lamech seventy times seven, four hundred and ninety, punishments were decreed. If Cain was unjust, if the judgment of God on Cain was just, so that Cain paid the seven penalties, for Cain did not learn how to murder from another. Lamech, on the other hand, saw Cain paying the penalty as a murderer, and he thought, although I have before my eyes Cain groaning and trembling and behold the magnitude of the wrath of God, I have not been chastened by his example; hence I deserve to pay four hundred and ninety punishments.

---

[21] Cf. Gn 4.14.   [22] Gn 4.15.
[23] Cf. Dn 12.2 (LXX).
[24] Cf. Gn 4.23. The quotation in Cyril is incomplete, the text is corrupt and several lines are omitted causing confusion but proving the letter is by Basil.

(12) Some interpreters have gone to such a point of reasoning, which is not inharmonious with ecclesiastical doctrine, that from Cain to the flood seven ages went past, and straightway the punishment was laid upon the earth because the outpouring of sin became great, but the guilt of Lamech was in need not of a flood for its cure, but had a need of him "who takes away the sin of the world."[25]

[25] Jn 1.29. Here the Greek text stops in Cyril's manuscript. The letter in Basil continues for several more pages.

LETTER 81

From a letter of the same, to the holy fathers at Scitis on account of those who object to the condemnation of the teachings of Origen.[1]

Some have dared to say that Origen was a teacher of the church. Is it fitting to put up with such people? If Origen is a teacher of the church, then the Arians, the Eunomians, and the pagans exult, some who blaspheme against the Son and the Spirit, and others who share their impiety and scoff at the resurrection of the dead. For it is clear from the statements that he who follows the holy Fathers does not doubt that those who side with Origen are following the aberration of the pagans and the madness of the Arians. Cyril among the saints, Bishop of Alexandria, from his letter to the monks at Phua, says these things against those who say that there is no resurrection of the body:

CCORDINGLY, THEY say that some of those among you deny the resurrection of human bodies, which is part of our confession of faith, made when we go forward to our saving baptism. When we are confessing the faith, we add that we also believe in the resurrection of the flesh. If we do away with this, and if we do not believe that Christ was raised from the dead, in order that he might raise us with him, we have a lame faith, and, having given up the royal road, we are traveling the twisted one.

(2) Such an evil doctrine is from the madness of Origen, which our Fathers publicly denounced and anathematized as perverting the truth. He did not think as a Christian, but wandered at random because he followed the nonsense of the pagans. The beginning of his error happened from this. He

---

[1] For the critical text of this letter see Schwartz, *ACO* 3 pp. 201–202. Geerard numbers this letter 5381 in *CPG*. These are parts of a letter by Cyril against the errors of Origen which are quoted in *Justiniani Edictum Contra Origenem*.

says that our souls existed earlier than our bodies, and from holiness were carried away unto evil desires, and revolted from God, and because of this guilt he condemned them and embodied them, and they are in flesh as in a prison.

(3) But the church, following the divinely inspired Scriptures, does not know a soul existing before the body, nor that the soul sinned before the body. How was that which did not subsist able also to sin? We say that the creator of all things fashioned the body from the earth, and animated it with a rational soul. And this is the constitution of man.

[And, after other passages:]

(4) That the soul of man was not condemned for sins committed before the existence of the body, as they say, and sent down into this world, the all-wise Paul will testify writing, "For all of us must be made manifest before the tribunal of Christ, so that each one may receive what he has won through the body, according to his works, whether good or evil."[2] Why does he say that we must be made manifest only through the acts of the body, and not rather through the acts before the body also, if he knew that the soul pre-existed and sinned before being in the body?

(5) If we are judged for only those things done through the body, obviously we do not have sin before existence of the body, for the soul of man did not at all subsist before him. Even the meaning of the letter of the law fully confirms us in this. If, as Origen says after he has wandered into error, the soul received the body by reason of a punishment, or retribution, for sins committed before the existence of the body, for what reason does the law threaten death for those who sin? It would be necessary rather that they just die, in order that they might be freed from the bonds of the body and the retribution, but it would be necessary that criminals live, in order that they might be punished by not being released from the bonds of the body.

[2] 2 Cor 5.10.

LETTER 82

To my lord, beloved brother and fellow bishop, Amphilochius, Bishop of Iconium, Cyril sends greetings in the Lord.[1]

KNOW THAT YOUR reverence, being very wise, will consider nothing better than charity and love toward brothers. Your reverence will consider a skillfully done action the best prudence in all things which are to be done. Therefore I write to your reverence the words of love, requesting also what you know how to do, so that it is plain that strong and very bitter words are not to be used with regard to those who desire to repent, and to desert the most unholy heresy of the Messalians, that is, the Euchites,[2] and to hurry toward the true teachings of the church.

(2) It is sufficient for those going in this direction to confess, "I anathematize the heresy of the Messalians, that is, the Euchites." He who very finely, even after this, offers them perhaps passages read aloud from books, disturbs men who do not have great precision of mind. Many are uneducated and are thus not able to reason in such a way that they would condemn thoroughly what is worthy of condemnation. Accordingly it is sufficient that they anathematize the heresy. Let them not be offered words in order that the love of argument on the part of some because of their lack of education[3] may

[1] For the critical text of this letter see Schwartz, *Codex vaticanus gr. 1431*, p. 20. Geerard numbers this letter 5382 in *CPG*. The date of this letter is probably prior to 427.

[2] For the Greek text of the definition against the Messalians or Euchites, see Schwartz, *ACO* 1.1.7 pp. 117–118.

[3] The heresy was first condemned at the Council of Side in 390 over which Amphilocius of Iconium presided. They were then apparently illiterate. They were again condemned at the Council of Ephesus in 431. See Quasten 3.163–164, 297.

not frequently drive them away even from desiring to believe rightly.

(3) I write these words, not to show favor to some, but rather because I know that charity in these matters is best. Precision for the most part disturbs many even of those who are the wisest.

LETTER 83

To Calosyrius, Bishop of Arsinoe, against those saying God is anthropomorphic.[1]

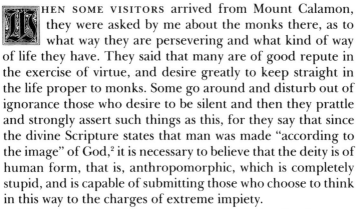HEN SOME VISITORS arrived from Mount Calamon, they were asked by me about the monks there, as to what way they are persevering and what kind of way of life they have. They said that many are of good repute in the exercise of virtue, and desire greatly to keep straight in the life proper to monks. Some go around and disturb out of ignorance those who desire to be silent and then they prattle and strongly assert such things as this, for they say that since the divine Scripture states that man was made "according to the image" of God,[2] it is necessary to believe that the deity is of human form, that is, anthropomorphic, which is completely stupid, and is capable of submitting those who choose to think in this way to the charges of extreme impiety.

(2) Accordingly, it is true, and indeed admittedly, that man was made "according to the image" of God, but the likeness is not bodily. God is incorporeal. The Savior himself will teach us this, saying, "God is spirit."[3] Therefore he is not corporeal, if he is a spirit, nor is he in a form of a body. That which is without a body, would be also without the outward appearance of a body. The deity is without quantity and without visible form. If they think that God, who is over all, was endowed with form according to the nature of the human body,

---

[1] The Greek text is in P. E. Pusey, *Sancti Patris Nostri Cyrilli Archiepiscopi Alexandrini in D. Joannis Evangelium. Accedunt Fragmenta Varia Necnon Tractatus ad Tiberium Diaconum Duo* (Oxford: At the Clarendon Press, 1872), 3:603–607. Geerard numbers this letter 5383 in *CPG*. See also Wickham, *Select Letters*, 214–221.

[2] Cf. Gn 1.26.   [3] Jn 4.24.

let them say whether he also has feet, in order that he may walk about, hands, in order that he may work with them, and eyes, in order that he may see through them. To what place does he go? From which places to which places does he travel, who fills all things? He said, "Do I not fill both heaven and earth?"[4] Which hands does he, who creates through the living Word, move to work?[5] If he has eyes, as we do, situated in the face, doubtless he does not at all see whatever is behind him. When he looks toward the East, he does not know what those in the West are doing. If he looks toward the West in turn, he does not see those in the East.

(3) I am ashamed to write these words, but through the senselessness of some men I have become witless, not willingly, but rather forced by them. Accordingly, let those who chatter about these things be refuted as ignorant and let them be quiet without handling matters above their powers, or rather let them not speak against God. God is above every creature, nor is he thought of as a body, nor in types, or appearances. He is simple, immaterial, without form, not compounded, not of parts, or limbs put together out of parts, as we are, but, on the other hand, he is spirit,[6] according to the Scriptures, and oversees all things, since he is everywhere, and fills all things, and never departs from anything, for he fills heaven and earth.[7]

(4) The fact that man was made according to the image of God[8] has other meanings and significations. Man, alone among all the living creatures on the earth, is rational, compassionate, has a tendency toward every virtue, and has assigned to him rule over all things upon the earth, in "the image and likeness" of God. Accordingly, as man is a rational, living being, and insofar as he loves virtue, and has power over the things on earth, it is stated that he has been made in the image of God.

(5) If they think the image of God is said to be according to the form of the body, nothing keeps them from saying that

[4] Jer 23.24.   [5] Cf. Jn 1.3.
[6] Cf. Jn 4.24.   [7] Jer 23.24.
[8] Cf. Gn 1.26.

God is of the same form as the irrational group of living things. We see that they are of the same parts as we, having feet, eyes, nostrils, tongue and the rest of the limbs of the body. Let your reverence, therefore, stop such men and, even more, reprove those accustomed to such chatterings.

(6) I hear that they say that the sacred consecration is of no avail unto sanctification if a fragment might remain unto another day. They are insane who say these things. Christ is not altered, nor is his holy body changed, but the power of the consecration and his life-giving grace is perpetual in his body.

(7) There are some other men going about, as they say, pretending only to devote themselves to prayer[9] and doing no work, and making piety a pretext for cowardice and a means of gaining a living, but not thinking rightly. Let them say that they are better even than the holy apostles who worked when opportunity gave them time for it, and they were wearied out for the Word of God. How did they miss reading the holy Paul writing to certain men, "For I hear that some among you are living irregularly, doing no work but busy at meddling."[10] The church does not admit those who do this. It is necessary without doubt that those who live a quiet life in the monasteries pray continually, but it does no harm and rather is exceedingly helpful to work in order that he who accepts the labors of others for his own need may not be found to be burdensome for others. It might be possible from his labors to relieve the widow and the orphan and some of the weak ones of his brethren.

(8) If they consider it a fine thing not to touch work, since they are striving after the same thing, who is the one feeding them? Some are making their idea, that it is necessary only to devote themselves to prayer and not to touch work at all, a pretext for laziness and gluttony.

(9) It is not possible for the orthodox to associate with the so-called Melitians[11] in order that they may not come into communion with their apostasy. If they, by changing over,

[9] The Euchites. See Quasten 3.163–165 and Cyril's Letter 82.
[10] Cf. 2 Thes 3.11.
[11] The followers of Melitius, Bishop of Lycopolis in Egypt. His name is

come toward the orthodox, let them be accepted. Let no one be negligent. Let no one be in communion with them, unless they change their minds, so that, as I said, the orthodox may not be in communion with their evil teaching.

(10) Let your reverence see to it that this letter be read in those monasteries unto the edification of those who are there, and let your reverence order that it be observed, so that the orthodox may not be afflicted by their consciences being enfeebled. Let those who desire to be nourished without work not have any loophole of appearing to be upright.

(11) I pray that you are well in the Lord, my beloved and most desired brother.

---

often spelled "Meletius." See *ODCC*², s.v., "Melitian Schisms." The sect was fading in Cyril's day.

LETTER 84

Cyril, to his most reverend and most desired brother and fellow bishop, Euoptius, greetings in the Lord.[1]

READ THE LETTER sent by your reverence and I have admired the disposition and the reality of your love in Christ. I understand that it is now necessary to say that what is said in the book of Proverbs is true, "a brother that is helped by his brother, is like a strong city."[2] It seems to me that the possession of love is worthy of every word about it in the divinely inspired Scripture, and very rightly, for it has the fullness of law, excels other virtues, and is held in high esteem in the souls of the saints. Yet we say that it is fulfilled not in bare and solitary utterances of words, but is testified by deeds themselves.

(2) Just as the most expensive of gems, which we say are Indian, are admired by those who see them, not from the things which someone might relate about them, but because of what they are, in the same way, I think, the brilliant beauty of love is manifested, when it is proved in all excellent ways by the upright themselves. Your reverence esteems it highly as you proceed in the way of the wisdom of the saints and imitate the glory of their good living in your own.

(3) I also welcomed now, as a full assurance of the disposition towards me which is in your reverence, the book that was

---

[1] For the critical text of this letter see Schwartz, *ACO* 1.1.6 pp. 110–111. It is the preface to Cyril's work against the twelve chapters by Theodoret. Theodoret's work, against the anathemas of Cyril in Letter 17, is now lost. The letter has to be dated in the earlier part of 431; cf. Quasten 3.127, 537. Geerard numbers this letter 5384 in *CPG*.

[2] Prov 18.19 (LXX).

delivered, which Theodoret of Cyrrhus, for they say that the little town is named in that way, is said to have composed against the anathemas.[3]

(4) After I read the contents, I raised hymns of thanks to God, not omitting to say this also, "Lord, deliver me from unjust lips and a tongue of cunning."[4] I find myself everywhere being falsely accused, and undergoing this in each of the chapters. I have understood that, as some of his associates say, the man is not without practice when it comes to speaking, and he has assembled without doubt no moderate knowledge of the Sacred Scriptures. Yet he has been carried away so far from knowing the meaning of the chapters that I think and believe hereafter that he is pleasing the desires of some people by pretending to be ignorant of it, so that he may not be considered to have used revilings against us rudely and excessively, but rather opportunely, although there is nothing hard to understand or high-sounding, as I think, in all our statements.

(5) But since it was necessary, although we have already written about these matters, to say a few things even against him, in order that someone may not think we have chosen to be silent because we have been condemned, I shall make my defense, speaking briefly. Therefore, it was necessary that he, being practiced in the divinely inspired Scriptures, if it was at all his intent to fashion arguments with us concerning the divine mysteries, merely to mention the Sacred Scriptures and thus to weave his tale as befits a holy man, and not bring into our midst ancient and foul myths. He sees fit to liken my words to the apple of discord, doubtless making the action be a display of the wisdom which is in him. Wherefore we also have held what concerns him in the greatest, and equally large, astonishment. He seems from his exceedingly great erudition and love of learning not ignorant of the apple of discord, nor indeed that the son of Priam was Paris.[5]

---

[3] Cf. note 1.   [4] Ps 119(120).2.

[5] The "apple of discord" was the prize for beauty at the wedding of Peleus, a mortal, and Thetis, a goddess, which caused contention between Hera, Athena and Aphrodite. So that Paris would award it to Aphrodite, she bribed

LETTER 84   115

(6) Yet, setting such matters aside for the present, we will cleave rather to the purpose set before us.

---

him with the promise that he would have Helen of Troy as his wife. The result was the Trojan War.

LETTER 85

Cyril, to his most venerable and most holy brethren and fellow bishops, Aurelius, Valentinus, and to all the most holy synod assembled in Carthage, greetings to your love in the Lord.[1]

ITH ALL JOY I received through our son, Innocent,[2] the priest, what was written by your honor with great piety. Since these writings were expected by us, with the result that we would send your charity from the register of our church the truest copies of the authentic synod at Nicaea, a city of Bithynia, that is, the things decreed and confirmed by the holy Fathers, underneath the confession of our faith, I considered it necessary, my lords, my most honored brethren,[3] since my affection guided me, to send to your charity through the same person, our son, Innocent, the priest, the most authentic copies which pertain to the synod at Nicaea, a city of Bithynia, which also you will find if you look for it in the ecclesiastical history.

(2) Concerning the Pasch, as you wrote, we announce to you that we will celebrate it on the day before the seventeenth of the Kalends of May in the coming indiction.[4]

---

[1] For the critical text of this letter see Joannou, *Fonti: Fascicolo IX: Discipline générale antique (IVe–IXe s)*, vol. 1, 2: *Les canons des synodes particuliers,* Pontificia commissione per la redazione del codice di diritto canonico orientale (Grottaferrata [Rome]: Tipografia Italo-Orientale "S. Nilo," 1962, 422–424. Geerard numbers this letter 5385 in *CPG*. Another version of this letter translated from Latin is in Appendix V.

[2] Innocent, the priest, was the messenger who delivered the letters.

[3] Aurelius was Bishop of Carthage from c. 391 to c. 430. See *ODCC*[2], s.v., "Aurelius." Valentinus was abbot of the monastery at Hadrumetum south of Carthage.

[4] The correct date may be ninth Kalends of May (April 23). An indiction was a period of fifteen years. Papadopoulos, *Ho Hagios Kurillos*, 452, dates this letter as before 428.

The Signature.

(3) May our God and Lord protect your holy synod; this we pray, most honored brethren.

LETTER 86
(Spurious) [1]

EAREST BROTHERS, this is what we desire that at the
same time we may celebrate the Pasch on the ninth
Kalends of May because of the calculation of the intercalary year. But if you would make it the seventh Kalends of
April, the twenty-second moon, as you are preparing to do,
you are making an ordinary year from an intercalary year,
while you observe that the moon was full on the third Nones
of March according to the Latin rule; for the Kalends of January, a Sunday, [is] the twenty-seventh moon. And it should not
be observed in this year for the reasons which we stated above.
Just as, moreover, we must avoid the Pasch, as we said, in this
year, so there must be caution, lest we make the Pasch of an
intercalary year be in an ordinary year, and [the Pasch] of an
ordinary year be in an intercalary year.

(2) For we ought to investigate the lunar epacts in the months
of an entire year, so that we may celebrate the Pasch in the
moon of the first month in the start of the year after the beginning of spring.[2] For the sun itself daily, on land and on sea
alike, both sets at the end of the day and rises at the beginning
of day. And the sun ends the course of an entire year on the
twelfth Kalends of April, and the fullness of the lunar globe
or its waning is foreseen by the motion of the fingers under
the guidance of reason and the variation in the measurement

---

[1] For the Latin text of this letter see Bruno Krusch, *Studien zur christlich-
mittelalterlichen Chronologie: Der 84 Jährige Ostercyclus und seine Quellen* (Leipzig,
1880), 345–349. The text of this spurious letter is attached without syntactic
interruption to the end of Appendix 5 of this book. Krusch condemns it as
spurious, as do Quasten 3.131 and Geerard, 5386 in *CPG*. It originated in
Ireland at the start of the seventh century A.D.

[2] That is, at the beginning of the Hebrew year.

with the aid of a method of calculation, so that we count only twelve moons according to the reckoning of the Law of the Hebrews in an ordinary year and thirteen in an intercalary year according to the reckoning of days.

(3) Moreover, I will point out to you that Pachomius, an outstanding monk, remarkable for deeds of apostolic grace and founder of the cenobites of Egypt, published letters at the monastery which in the Egyptian language is called Baum,[3] which he received at the dictation of an angel, so that they might not run into error in Paschal solemnities by calculation, and would know the moon of the first month in an ordinary year and in an intercalary year.

(4) My most dear lords, bear in mind that the Pasch was first instituted in Egypt to urge the sons of Israel to eat the lamb, as a symbol of the true Lamb, in the [full] moon of the first month. Later, however, the Pasch was celebrated as a remembrance of when the manna descended, which showed that the foreshadowing lamb would go away when the true Manna would descend.

(5) However, our Lord Jesus Christ joined on one day the lamb of the Jews and the true Manna, when he blessed bread and wine saying, "This is my body, and my blood,"[4] in the moon of the first month at the beginning of the year. Therefore, let us commemorate and let us be mindful to offer what Jesus offered for us in the first month. For the Lord Jesus said, "As often as you will do these things, you shall do them in remembrance and memory of me."[5]

(6) You should scrutinize most diligently what the Nicene synod ordained, fourteen moons of all the years through a nineteen year cycle, so that we would not be in error about the moon of the first month and would celebrate the Pasch on the following Sunday, and not make it on the fourteenth moon with the Jews and the heretics who are called Quartodecimans.[6]

(7) And it has been decreed in all synods, except the synods

[3] Variant readings given in Krusch are: *bauum, bonum, pabum,* and *pannum.*
[4] Cf. Mt 26.26–28.   [5] Cf. Lk 22.19 and 1 Cor 11.25.
[6] Cf. Quasten 1.77, 243, 246 and 3.340.

at Gangra and Caesarea, that no church, or state, or any re-
gion, should act contrary to these things which were decreed
about the Pasch at the Nicene Council. Believe me, since, if
the Nicene synod had not written, the lunar cycle of the first
month, the cycle of the Selinite stone in Persis would suffice as
an example of the Paschal reckoning, the inner whiteness of
which increases and decreases with the moon of the first
month.[7]

(8) Accordingly, I have announced to you all these matters
because you were in doubt about the moon of the first month
in this year. Accordingly, I enjoin you not to celebrate the
Pasch in the month of March in an intercalary year, but on
the ninth Kalends of May so that, in unity with the universal
church, we, true immaculate Israelites, may eat the immaculate lamb, because the command was given to carnal Israel to
eat the yearling lamb in one house.[8] Concerning that most
true immaculate Lamb it was commanded, "You shall not kill
a lamb in the milk of his mother,"[9] that is, in the next Pasch of
its conception in the womb of its mother.

(9) So, Joseph wished secretly to put away Mary who was
with child,[10] lest she be killed with stones as defiled and an
adulteress. In order that the lamb be not killed in the milk of
his mother, by an invisible teacher instructing Joseph, or lest
he be killed on the next Pasch of his nativity, Joseph fled into
Egypt by the command of an angel[11] in the month of March
as the year came round, in the month in which Cain led the
just Abel into the field[12] to kill him, as a prefiguration of
Christ, who was led to the tribunal of Pilate on the sixth day of
the week, because he died on the cross on the same day on
which he was conceived in the womb, while Adam died in
spirit on the sixth day of the week for sin in paradise and died
in his body on the same day.

---

[7] See *S. Aurelii Augustini De Civitate Dei* 21.5–29.32, ed. B. Dombart and
A. Kalb, CCL 48.765, and *Isidori Hispalensis Etymologiae*, ed. W. M. Lindsay
(Oxford: At the Clarendon Press, 1911), 16.4.6.

[8] Cf. Ex 12.46.   [9] Cf. Ex 23.19.
[10] Cf. Mt 1.19.   [11] Cf. Mt 2.13–15.
[12] Cf. Gn 4.8.

(10) A reply has been made, as I think, concerning all the matters which you have asked me, and I brought forth all the authentic documents of the Nicene synod to Innocent, the priest, so that he would bring them to you.

(11) Peace be with your spirit and mine in Jesus Christ, our Lord.

LETTER 87
(Spurious)

The beginning of the Prologue of Saint Cyril, Bishop of Alexandria, concerning the calculation of the Pasch.[1]

ET THE SACRED mystery of the Pasch and its brilliant solemnity be observed as it was handed down by our Savior to the apostles; it would have been unimpaired, if the perversity of some had not defiled it among other holy things of the faith.

(2) Those also who tried to reply because of their depravity and constructed a Paschal cycle of eighty-four years would have kept a cycle of perfect calculation, if in the computation of months or years they had been able to follow a human or divine tradition. Wherefore, they were involved in such darkness of ignorance, that they fell into both dangers of ignorance of the Pasch.

(3) So also from the fourteenth moon, which ordinary people think is the sixteenth, when still the circle of its orb had been filled up, by celebrating the Pasch on the evening of the Sabbath before the month of new fruits[2] they are shown to have erred frequently against the precept of the Lord.

---

[1] For the Latin text of this letter see Krusch, *Chronologie*, 337–343. Geerard numbers this letter 5387 in *CPG* but mentions in a cross reference to 5242, part of an appendix to Cyril's *Homilies*, that some scholars have denied its authenticity, and that even Krusch had doubts. See Krusch, *Chronologie*, 89–98 and E. Dekkers and E. Gaar, *Clavis Patrum Latinorum*, 2d ed. (Steenbrugge, 1961), 2291. The letter was condemned as spurious by Quasten 3.131. See also Charles W. Jones, *The Cyrillan Easter Table* in *Bedae opera de temporibus* (Cambridge, Mass.: The Medieval Academy of America, 1943), 34–54. Jones discusses a recension of the *Prologus Cyrilli*, which he names the *Chartres Praefatio*, found in Chartres MS 70 (saec. IX). However, he shows that Cyril did not compose it; see pp. 44 and 46.

[2] *mensem novorum*, see Ex 23.15 and Dt 16.1, Septuagint.

(4) Others, seeing this and rejecting it and, so to speak, wishing to correct it, because they were not illuminated by the divine revelation, but were puffed up by the presumption of human learning, produced something worse, so that they have attempted to describe different inextricable cycles, just as those do through six quattuordecennities,[3] so also those through seven sedecennities[4] and certain projections of measurements, by noting doubled and multiplied numbers and sketches.

(5) Through their difficulties, subtle and endless controversies in which they attack each other, some distinguished men have been offended so that they now, abandoning all observations, irrationally celebrate on the eighth day of the Kalends of April, no matter what moon or weekday it falls on, not the Pasch of the Lord, which is a solemnity on the day of the Resurrection and the fullness of light in the moon and the company of the everlasting sun, but merely the birthday of the world. Superfluously, however, did anyone extend human ingenuity and have a polished tongue, unless his perception would be guided to true wisdom by him who has made foolish the wisdom of this world.[5]

(6) Therefore, since by these and similar dissensions throughout the whole world the Paschal calculation would be disturbed, it was decreed by the advice of the synod[6] of the holy men of the whole world that, since the Church of Alexandria was found to be brilliant in this knowledge, every single year it should indicate by a letter to the Church of Rome on which Kalends or Ides, and in which moon, the Pasch should be celebrated, whence with apostolic authority the universal church throughout the whole world would know the definite day of the Pasch without any dispute.

(7) Since through many ages they observed this only partly and no one, therefore, believed any Scripture where no questions would be solved, and sometimes it happened that they were afraid to celebrate the Pasch on the Sabbath, the twen-

---

[3] Six times fourteen or 84 years.　　[4] Seven times sixteen or 112 years.
[5] Cf. 1 Cor 1.20.　　[6] At Nicaea.

tieth moon rather than the twenty-third, from the fifteenth of
the Kalends of May to the eighth of the same Kalends, as if
in a second month, and there was great confusion in every
church, praetorium or palace, Theodosius, the most religious
emperor, who was zealous to please God always, not only in
human, but also in divine laws, by his letter begged Theophilus, the Bishop of the entire city of Alexandria,[7] that he
write a treatise about the sacred feast of the Pasch by a most
evident calculation and deign to send it to him.

(8) Observing his most holy commands Theophilus instituted a Paschal cycle of four hundred and eighteen years for
his clemency, calculating from the first year of his consulship
onward to one hundred years, he determined for his subjects
by a letter on which Kalends or Ides, and in which moon, the
Pasch ought to be celebrated, and he faithfully and briefly enjoined the manifest truth by his letter.[8] In this, by the Lord
revealing it to him, he perfectly revealed the order of the calculation, and wiped out and dissolved all errors and superfluous questions more clearly than light.

(9) But, because now those different cycles, disseminated
throughout the whole world had unshakenly possessed our
minds, he who recently was published,[9] scarcely was able to
reach a few. When I had seen his extreme profundity ex-
ceeded almost all perceptions, I requested a revelation of the
Lord. Relying on it I have explained in this little book what I
have deserved to draw from the very fountain, which I knew
they, among whom I saw the cycle itself, have not understood.
And lest by chance the unending accumulation of four-hun-
dred and eighteen years cause to some a dislike in compre-
hending it, or a sluggishness in describing it, I have shortened
that same cycle to ninety-five years, which cycle I knew ran
without any difference through those years. I have warned
that only one unit be added, or rather taken away, in certain
years because of the calculation of the intercalary day, which

[7] Cyril's uncle and predecessor.
[8] This claim, that Theodosius asked for and agreed to a table of Theophilus, is false. See Quasten 3.102.
[9] Theophilus.

could not occur until that final year of the cycle, which returns at the start.

(10) Affirming that the sacred Pasch is celebrated from the twelfth Kalends of April to the seventh Kalends of May, through thirty-five days, which makes five weeks, which now, it is plain, have the other five days of the week itself, he added that, because of the Lord's day, it would extend from the fourteenth moon to the twenty-first, as was enjoined. This moon becomes, indeed, the nineteenth from the twelfth day of the Kalends of April to the fourteenth Kalends of May. And, therefore, I have not hesitated to extend these five days, because that very moon, extended to the seventh Kalends of May, is foreknown later than the ends of the first month, is filled up and, according to the reckoning of the Hebrews, upon whom the Pasch was enjoined as a prefigurement of Christ, occurs after the intercalary year, which was divinely revealed to holy Moses to have thirteen lunar months, that is three hundred and eighty-four days. Whence it is evident that these five added days of the month of new fruits are not of the second month, but of the first, which days even if they were of the second month, because of the Resurrection of the Lord and the plenitude of the church would seem to be added not undeservedly.

(11) Those who also lived farther off, or had been unclean in soul, were commanded to celebrate the Pasch in the second month,[10] which is understood as a type of the holy church, which, since she has been defiled by all demons, was seen to be unclean in soul, but cleansed by a saving confession, is commanded to pass over unto a second birth, as if to a second month. However, before the month of new fruits is the last old month, in which it is completely forbidden that the true Pasch be held.

(12) But in order that I may state briefly the things in which their calculation is different: the moon which they improperly call the third, or sixteenth, or the twenty-third, this moon the holy Theophilus affirms is the first, or the fourteenth, or

[10]Cf. Nm 9.13.

the twenty-first, with heaven proving it. Moreover, the Pasch which they fear to celebrate beyond the twelfth Kalends of May the holy Theophilus did not hesitate to postpone up to the seventh Kalends of May. In the calculation of those years some added one lunar day from the lunar increments in the fourteenth year, others in the sixteenth year. The holy Theophilus added this day in the nineteenth year. Hence, their calculation runs ahead, because it is improper and different, but his prevails, because it is founded on truth and endures forever. For thus Theophilus wishes to see the fourteenth moon in the sky, so that it would rise in the full circle of its orb at the same moment at which the sun sets and, when that same night has passed by, the sun should rise when the moon is setting. Wherefore, it evidently appears that the moon which they, as the twenty-third, fear to observe on the Sabbath of the Pasch, he, affirming it was the twenty-first, decided without any fear that the holy Pasch be celebrated, and the other one which they falsely anticipate as the fifteenth after the Sabbath has passed, he, by showing it was the thirteenth, and contending that they were not celebrating it rightly, did not hesitate to bring it down to the twenty-first.

(13) Moreover, it is obvious that the moon has twenty-nine and one half days, and when this is doubled, the days make fifty-nine. To these one more day than those two halves is added, so that they seem to make sixty, and a legitimate lunar increment is produced, so that, if nominally it would be the fifth moon, by another day it would be called, not the sixth but the seventh. Moreover, none of the calculators is ignorant of the fact that the thirtieth moon has a half of waning and a half of increasing, and hence the one which is called the thirtieth is the one which is the first. Therefore, such a moon ought to be seen as the twenty-ninth, as after the day before at evening it ought to be the first. However, the thirtieth moon is not able to be seen at all, because, at the very end, it is spent in the middle of the thirtieth day, and is in conjunction with the sun, and in the same moment it is reborn, receding little by little from it, and through the remaining part of that very thirtieth day, all the way to the next day, which is called the

first, it increases, so that it is seen after the setting of the sun, just as the twenty-ninth is seen at dawn on the day before, as I said earlier. What blindness of mind, therefore, it is, or madness, that, although the thirtieth cannot be seen, it still is seen to be waning, and is called the first, and sometimes even the second? As if they were telling lies through the entire calculation! For just as they call the moon the second, instead of the thirtieth, and the third instead of the first, so they are forced to say the sixteenth instead of the fourteenth, and the twenty-third instead of the twenty-first. So, to have found the smallness of that which is called the intercalary day, so that through this fallacy the devil would catch Christian souls among the very holy things of the faith.

(14) Likewise this cites the highest and insuperable precedent, the fact that our Savior celebrated the Pasch with his disciples on the fourteenth moon, on the fifth day of the week, and commanded that it be done so always.[11] This is celebrated today, as it was handed down, and the holy chrism is made ready, and the supper of the Lord is fulfilled with yearly solemnity, which is the perfect Pasch and the greatest sacrament, as the holy apostle relates that it was handed down to him and glories that it was handed down to the Corinthians.[12] On the fourteenth he was betrayed, and on the fifteenth he suffered, and on the seventeenth he rose, that is to say, on that moon which, with no darkness intervening even according to the calculation of ordinary people, is associated with the dawn by the light of the sun. For this truly is the sign of salvation that, leaving behind us the darkness of all wickedness, we enjoy the light of the sun by that eternal sun.

(15) Therefore, if you subtract these superfluous two days of the moon, you will understand those five days of the month of new fruits added according to the calculation, but also if you should add that day from the lunar increments to the nineteen years, not to the fourteen or the sixteen, you would recognize all the force and the calculation of the truth of this

[11] Cf. Lk 22.19 and 1 Cor 11.24. See R. Ginns, "The Gospel of Jesus Christ according to St. Luke," *CCHS*, sections 768b, 965–966.
[12] Cf. 1 Cor 11.23–27.

mystery. However, the moon, which is called the third by these men, today is called the first by the Jews and the pagans, and rightly it is seen at evening, because it also already has a half of the thirtieth, which also is equally the first.

Also the calculation of the course of the sun or moon
and the intercalary day.

(16) The year has three hundred and sixty-five days, twelve months, four seasons: spring, summer, autumn and winter. And through the four seasons there are two equinoxes and two solstices. On the ninth Kalends of April is one equinox, and on the eighth Kalends of July, on the birthday of Saint John,[13] is one solstice, and on the eighth Kalends of January, on the birthday of our Lord Jesus Christ, is another solstice.

(17) For the sun also shines three hundred and sixty-five and one quarter days in a year, but the moon shines three hundred and fifty-four days. The remaining eleven are those on which the sun is seen to shine, as above. And these eleven are those which are added to the course of the moon every year. And so that the calculation be manifested more clearly: there are twelve months in a year and there are seven of these months which have more than thirty days each, that is, January, March, May, July, August, October, December. And, accordingly, take away one day each from December and January and add them to February which has twenty-eight days, and they become thirty days. But take away those remaining days, which in the beginning add more than the number thirty to five months, and all are equal, so that they have thirty days.

(18) And one lunar month appears, twenty-eight and one half days, as already we have said before in the letter written above, because it does not involve a thirtieth day. Accordingly, there are twelve lunar months in the year, but through each lunar month it appears less by one half each time. And accordingly, from twelve lunar months take away twelve halves

[13] John the Baptist.

and count them together and they make six days. To these add those five days from the five months and they make eleven days together, which seem to add to the course of the moon, because on them the moon shines less than the sun.

(19) However, the quarter, which is more than the three hundred and sixty-five days, makes an increase of an intercalary day every fourth year. But the quarter itself has three twelfths, which increase in one year. Likewise, in another year, three, in a third year three, in a fourth three, and they become together twelve hours, and they make one day, which is called the intercalary day. And so the other days, which make up the year, are added and subtracted, so that also, when the intercalary day comes every fourth year, a day, which comes in the calculation to make up that year, as the third weekday, must be subtracted and a fourth weekday must be reckoned. And thus the intercalary day is handed down by the tradition of our ancestors.

Here ends the Prologue of Saint Cyril, the Bishop of Alexandria.[14]

[14] For further information about the Easter controversy see Herbert Thurston, S. J., "Easter Controversy" in *The New Catholic Encyclopedia*, 5.228–230, and E. Schwartz, *Christliche und Jüdische Ostertafeln* in *Abhandlungen der königlichen Gesellschaft der Wissenschaften zu Göttingen*, Philosophisch-Historische Klasse, N.s., vol. 8, no. 6 (Berlin: Weidmannische Buchhandlung, 1905).

LETTER 88
(Spurious)

To blessed Cyril, the archbishop. A copy [of a letter] on a writing tablet by Hypatia who taught philosophy at Alexandria.[1]

EADING THE HISTORIES of the ages I found that the presence of Christ occurred one hundred and forty years ago.[2] There were disciples of his who afterwards were called apostles, who after his assumption into heaven preached the doctrine of Christ, who taught rather simply indeed and without any superfluous curiosity, so that many of the pagans, those poorly informed and those who are wise, found an opportunity to accuse this doctrine and call it inconsistent, for the evangelist said, "No one has at any time seen God."[3] How, therefore, they say, (do you say) that God was crucified? They say, how was he affixed to a cross, who has not been seen? How did he die, and how was he buried?

(2) Nestorius,[4] therefore, who recently was driven into exile, explained the preachings of the apostles. I, learning a long time ago that he confessed that there were two natures in Christ, say to him who had said these words, "the questions of the pagans are solved." Therefore, I say that your holiness has done wrong to him who holds teachings contrary to yours, to gather a synod and without opposition to have prepared to effect his deposition.

[1] For the critical text of this spurious letter see Schwartz *ACO* 1.4 p. 240. Geerard numbers this letter 5388 in *CPG*.
[2] At the supposed time of this letter the period would be about 440 years, not 140 years.
[3] Jn 1.18.
[4] Hypatia died in March 415, before Nestorius became Patriarch of Constantinople in 428 and before the start of the Nestorian heresy. The Council of Ephesus condemned him in 431.

(3) Within a few days, after inspecting the explanations of this same man and applying the apostolic preachings, and after thinking within myself that it would be good for me to become a Christian, I hope that I am made worthy of the regeneration of the Lord's baptism.

LETTER 89

Cyril, to my lord, my beloved brother and fellow bishop, John, greetings in the Lord.[1]

T O BE PARTAKERS in good things very greatly delights us and those who might be finding them, but it is even exceedingly painful in equal measure to seem to be bereft of them. May your excellency know that we have suffered this, for I was gladdened when I met with our most pious and most God-loving brother and fellow bishop, Paul,[2] and I marveled at the complete courtesy of the man, and I was hurt in no small measure, when he departed from Alexandria. And it was necessary that I, even unwilling, stand aside, since he desired to do this.

(2) Therefore, I shall indeed remember his most sweet association and affection, and I shall not have ceased admiring your holiness, because you exhorted a man accustomed to be highly esteemed to come to us, and have rendered him an admirer of your sagacity and us warmer admirers of your goodness.

---

[1] For the critical text of this letter to John of Antioch see Schwartz, *ACO* 1.1.7 p. 153. It was unknown until he published it. Lampe numbers this *ep.* 90 in *PGL*. Geerard numbers this letter 5389 in *CPG*. From the contents it belongs soon after Letter 39, the one celebrating the reconciliation in 433.

[2] Paul, Bishop of Emesa.

LETTER 90

Cyril, to my lord, my beloved brother and fellow bishop, John, greetings in the Lord.[1]

SINCE YOUR HOLINESS is all-wise and knows the ordinances of ecclesiastics, doubtless you thoroughly realize that some of the affairs are in our hands and others are in the hands of others, and that each of us manages his own church and has attached to himself the authority of the management of things being put in motion under him.

(2) Accordingly, since my lord, the most God-fearing Acacius, Bishop of Beroea, a man most happy in his old age, has written to those in Constantinople that my lord, our most God-fearing brother and fellow bishop, Paul,[2] was sent by your holiness to Alexandria, and since he has made this very thing known, my lord, the most God-fearing and most holy bishop, Maximian,[3] wrote to me straightway, exhorting me a very great deal about the necessity of soberly laying the foundations of the peace of the churches.

(3) He added that some have been condemned both by him and by the many other bishops who happened to be in the metropolis of Constantinople, and he wrote their names; I mean, Helladius of Tarsus, Eutherius of Tyana, Dorotheus of Marcianopolis, and Himerius of Nicomedia.[4]

---

[1] For the critical text of this letter to John of Antioch see Schwartz, *ACO* 1.1.7 pp. 153–154. It was unknown until he published it. Lampe numbers this *ep.* 91 in *PGL*. Geerard numbers this letter 5390 in *CPG*. From the contents it, like *CPG* 5389, belongs soon after Letter 39, the one celebrating the reconciliation in 433.

[2] Bishop of Emesa. He was the intermediary between John of Antioch and Cyril. See Letters 36 and 37.

[3] Bishop of Constantinople.   [4] See Letters 11 and 48.

(4) Then he added that, if I should lay claim to the case and should dismiss the decree passed against them, the arrangements of the peace will become completely lame. The expressions were near to threatening and placed an excommunication and very great unpleasantness between us and him, if any innovations were made on my part concerning this case.

(5) And in another manner, if one must tell the truth, neither did I receive the memoranda on the things done concerning them nor did I maintain the vote of deposition against any persons. We clearly know it and it was necessary, especially since the same most holy man signified that we should not lay claim to the matter.

(6) Accordingly, my lord, the most God-fearing bishop, Paul, was much wearied out by urging arguments on me about these matters. I said to his reverence what I have even now written to your holiness and added this, that, to speak in the presence of God, when peace comes, it will be possible thereafter to return confidently to our communion as now, or at least to dispatch our requests to Constantinople and employ them in their behalf, if indeed any manner of paying court will win the argument in the memoranda prepared concerning them. But I think he will not be sluggish towards the messages of those making the requests.

LETTER 91

Here begins a letter of blessed Cyril, to blessed John, Bishop of Antioch, and to the synod which assembled under him, for Theodore.[1]

 READ THE LETTER which your God-loving assembly by common consent addressed to me after common deliberation. And I judged it unnecessary to speak or write anything indeed about the beginning of the letter, and rightly, as I think. For I saw you, so to speak, panting and I, wholly stunned, passed on to this matter which was urging you on.

(2) For how would I not perceive in my mind the watchful zeal of you who have written, indeed I should add also the struggle which you all alike have undertaken for an admirable man and one deserving the greatest glory among you, I mean Theodore.[2]

(3) You cry out against those who hold themselves, as it seems, hostile towards him, and are making an opportunity for the opposite teaching by which they are held. They demanded that certain chapters, not understood by better men, as some have said, be condemned, and because of this they have disturbed your holiness. For this reason, moreover, as your letter shows, they are on the move proceeding to the

---

[1] For the critical text of this letter see Schwartz, *ACO* 1.5 pp. 314–315. In his introductory comment Schwartz states that by this letter Cyril was not replying to the preceding letter, which is Letter 66 in Cyril's collection, but to another one from John of Antioch written after it. Another Latin version is in J. Straub, *ACO* 4.1 (Berlin, 1971) pp. 105–106 where this letter is called a forgery. See Cyril's Letters 66, 67, 68, and 72. Geerard numbers this letter 5391 in *CPG*.

[2] Theodore of Mopsuestia. For the chapters or excerpts from his writings see Letter 66.

capital city,[3] to see if in any way they may prevail in persuad-
ing by a meeting of some persons that by an imperial action
those chapters may be subjected to an anathema, which are
produced by them along with an accusation against those willing to defend them. However, I speak to this point according
to what seems good to me and to everyone who has sense,
since it is wrong to consider or to treat harshly those who do
not know[4] how to walk aright and also to leave far off those
who think this way, unless by chance what they want to produce should be taken into consideration, most of all when the
person whom they put at fault is not at hand,[5] and the refutation of the chapters is uncertain and those who are engaged
in these matters are found running to an uncertain goal[6] and
beating the air.

(4) But, dismissing those subjects, I say this that there is
need, in whatever manner they come to teach or are disposed
to write, to examine with the total eye of the mind the understanding of the divine Scriptures and to proceed properly
with attention to them and thus to weigh their own books in
judgment, fearing lest by teaching and believing what is contrary to what is allowed they may be called the least in the
kingdom of heaven.[7] The desire for it[8] makes those who are
devoted to it flee the hindrances of the journey leading to it
and hasten toward that narrow [gate].[9]

(5) Moreover, briefly I will say to you, beloved of God, what
we have done, which was necessary because of your letters.
I clearly have written to the God-loving bishop of the capital city, Proclus, in these words: the explanation which was
produced at the holy synod at Ephesus as one set down by
Theodore, as those offering it had said, because it had nothing sound, the holy synod nullified indeed as full of perverse
ideas condemning, moreover, those who so thought, [but] ju-

---

[3] Constantinople.
[4] Schwartz notes that he printed *sciunt* according to the manuscript Σ but
that the manuscript *P* Fac. reads *nesciunt*.
[5] Theodore of Mopsuestia died in 428, before the Council of Ephesus
in 431.
[6] Cf. 1 Cor. 9.26.   [7] Cf. Mt 5.19.
[8] The kingdom of heaven.   [9] Cf. Mt 7.13, 14.

diciously did not make mention of the man, neither did it subject him by name to an anathema, nor did others for prudential reasons, as is thought, lest by chance due to the greater
honor of that man the Eastern [bishops] giving heed to it
might tear themselves away from the unity of the body of the
universal church and join the hateful and condemned faction and beget occasions of scandals for many others. For the
people love with great desire to subject their hearing to whatever opinions they like and, more quickly than one might say,
to depart from competent reasoning.

(6) But justly they, who furnish causes of this kind, will
hear, even if they do not wish it, "You forget yourselves when
you stretch your bows against a dead man, for he does not
survive who is inscribed among you." [10] And let no one blame
me that I have gone on in these words, but let them yield very
much to their most famed predecessor for it is a serious thing
to scoff at the dead, even if they were laymen, much less at
those who have laid down this life in the episcopacy. For it
seems the most just thing to prudent men to yield to the one
knowing beforehand the disposition of each one and knowing
of what sort each one will be.

The end of the letter of Cyril, Bishop of Alexandria, to John, the
bishop, in behalf of Theodore.

[10] The quotation has not been identified.

LETTER 91
(Alternate Version)

However, that fabricated letter is as follows:[1]

VIEWED THE LETTER in which your holiness spoke to me as from the common will of the synod assembled as one. And I thought it superfluous to say anything or to speak out indeed about the beginning of the letter, and very rightly. For when I saw you, as someone may say, aroused in spirit, and when I was greatly astounded, I hastened to do this which is necessary.

(2) For how would I not have been keeping in mind your so admirable and careful zeal, moreover, I should also add the struggle which you have entirely undertaken not only just for an admirable man but also for one who has gained the greatest glory among you, I mean Theodore.[2]

(3) You cry out against some who have, as it seems, a hatred against the man and make an opportunity for the impiety by which they are held, and, as some said, who have disturbed your reverence by demanding the rejection of certain erroneous chapters. For this reason even now, as your letter shows, going to the capital city[3] they cause disturbance, to see if in any way it may happen that they persuade by circumvention of some there that through imperial action these [chapters], which are proffered by them to incriminate their defenders,

[1] The Latin text of this alternate version of the letter is in J. Straub, *ACO*, 4.1 pp. 105–106. In the line which introduces the text it is called a forgery. It may well be that this version is spurious for the tone differs much from the text edited by Schwartz, as a comparison shows.
[2] Theodore of Mopsuestia. For the chapters or excerpts from his writings see Letter 66 of Cyril.
[3] Constantinople.

be anathemetized. And because of this, as it seems to me and to everyone having sense, it is not right to sadden or treat harshly those who think aright, but also to leave very far off those having a wish of that kind, I will not say also to have in mind what they have thought, most of all when the person whom they subject to blame is not certain, and moreover the refutation of the chapters is held to be uncertain, and now these who did this are found running to an uncertain goal[4] and beating the air.

(4) But, passing over these matters, I will say this, that it is proper that those, who in some manner are brought forward to teach or wish to write, behold with the sincere eye of the mind the understanding of divine Scripture and proceed rightly toward its intention and thus dispose their utterances unto judgment, fearing lest perhaps by teaching or thinking on the contrary the opposite to what it is, they may be called least in the kingdom of heaven,[5] the desire for which forces those who look toward it to reject wandering from the way which leads to that kingdom and to hasten to that blessed life.[6]

(5) Moreover, I will briefly say to you, most religious [brethren,] this also which I have written to Proclus, the most reverend Bishop of the city of Constantinople, satisfying your letter in the very words as follows: that when the exposition was brought forth at the holy council at Ephesus, as set down by Theodore, as they who brought it forth said, having nothing sound, indeed the holy council rejected it as being full of perverse ideas, condemning moreover those who so think, [but] judiciously made no mention of the man and did not anathematize him by name, nor indeed others for prudential reasons, as it seems, lest perhaps the Eastern [bishops] heeding the great estimation of the man with which he is admired, would separate themselves from communion with the universal church and add themselves to the hateful and condemned faction and beget occasions of scandal for the greatest number possible. For the people are accustomed to lend their ears

[4]Cf. 1 Cor 9.26.   [5]Cf. Mt 5.19.
[6]Cf. Mt 7.13,14.

with the greatest pleasure to what rumors they like and, more quickly than one might say, to depart from competent reason.

(6) But justly the authors of those rumors will hear, although they do not wish it, "You hide yourselves stretching your bows against a dead man, for he does not survive who is accused by you."[7] And let no one blame me that I have gone on in these words, but I yield to those thinking it is a serious thing to scoff at the dead, although they be laymen, how much the more also at those who departed from life in the episcopacy. For it is the part of prudent men to yield most justly to the one knowing beforehand the disposition of each one and knowing of what sort each one of us will become.

(7) May the Lord preserve you in all things, doing well and praying for us, most religious [brethren].

[7] The quotation has not been identified.

LETTER 92

Cyril, to my beloved brother and fellow bishop, Acacius, greetings in the Lord.[1]

ELIEVING THAT IT was rightly said by the blessed Paul, "Render to all men whatever is their due,"[2] I have not ceased as the opportunity came, so I persuade myself, to pay due and fitting respect properly to your holiness[3] even as in assessment of a debt, for it was necessary; it was necessary to do this and honor so august a white head continually with greetings.

(2) Since I have taken your counsel concerning every ecclesiastical and necessary matter, and in this I think that I know your most God-fearing mind, I have also often written about Nestorius that he confuses everything and greatly confounds the tranquillity of the churches by debasing the account of the apostolic and evangelical tradition, which is right and truly inviolable, by certain foreign and very novel inventions of reasoning.

(3) And indeed I received the writings from your holiness on this subject, written when you were almost weeping and, as if from foresight, looking with suspicion at the condition of affairs which is about to be in the future. And it was most clear to all beforehand that we have not summoned a council into existence, but he himself did it, one who laid the foundation of the disagreement in the beginning, the sower of weeds.[4]

---

[1] For the critical text of this letter see Schwartz, *ACO* 1.1.7 pp. 140–142. The letter was unknown until published by him. Geerard numbers it 5392 in *CPG*. Lampe numbers it *ep*. 89 in *PGL*. From its contents the letter belongs to the period after the deposition of Nestorius and the election of Maximian as Bishop of Constantinople, October 25, 431, that is, following Letter 32.

[2] Rom 13.7.　　　　　　　　　　　　　[3] Acacius of Beroea.
[4] Cf. Mt 13.25.

(4) I did not write first to the Church of Rome concerning him, but rather he himself began this also. When we were counselling him to refrain from blasphemies against Christ and rather think the truth with us, he, following his own reasoning, putting together his distorted explanations and long letters, sent them to my lord, the most God-fearing and most pious Bishop of the Church of Rome, Celestine. After reading the writings and the explanations, he condemned him as like to one stammering, or rather like to one saying certain impious and discordant things against Christ, the Savior of us all. As a result he issued a definition against him and also wrote to me to remind him again through letters, so that he would refrain from his evil teaching and choose instead to be eminent in pressing forward in the true faith.

(5) And, in order that I may not seem tiresome to your holiness by spending a number of words on this subject, I will go again to the point. We have fully narrated the manner in which the holy council was brought together in the city of Ephesus, and I say this once, namely, that I thought your holiness completely agreed that the council did not assemble about some of those random things which happen, but about the true faith itself and the condition of all the churches. I continued receiving even in Ephesus itself along with all the other most God-fearing bishops reports such as these, that your reverence will come, and is at hand, and has announced that you are doing this, but perhaps very many things came to be in the way, and more important than other reasons your august and honorable age and the weakness of your body.

(6) But when those from the East who are near you, announced it, I learned with reluctance that your excellency declined to come. When the most God-fearing bishops had gathered together from the whole Roman empire, as it were, and each one was troubled at the extension of days and saying that his own church and city was held back from progressing, since there were many heretics in each one, and indeed that other perversions were occurring, then how was it possible for me to write to your holiness from such distances as Ephesus to ask your pardon?

(7) I could not [write], either, by a swift soldier running, for we did not have a man serving us for this purpose, nor by a cleric who could endure the time away from home to go and return, for there was a very great throng of those who were distraught, as I said, and I already communicated with your holiness about all these matters even before I went abroad from Alexandria. Let your holiness, therefore, not think that I am so heedless of the proper thing as to choose to be silent about matters so very necessary.

(8) I have been grieved exceedingly about the things which happened at the council, for some of those from the East carried around a copy of a letter, as if written by your holiness against me to the most pious emperor, and the pattern of the letter was this, that the Bishop of Alexandria, because he had a hatred toward Nestorius, contrived a plot against him, and other things having the same impact as these.

(9) If the letter is one from your holiness, rightly have I been grieved, as I think, for what personal hatred do I find that I have had toward Nestorius? For when he had been consecrated,[5] immediately I wrote messages of communion and sent a letter to him full of praise, for I did not know what was to be, and then the entire discussion against him happened, not about a common matter in my eyes but about the true faith alone.

(10) But if some people fabricated the letter, they will defend themselves before God, because they have disparaged your holiness and have made me be blamed for silence and for your pain. That the holy council in the city of Ephesus did nothing out of place or anything beyond what was fitting or anything beyond proper reason, can be seen from the acts themselves. For we did not sit in council about someone ordinary, nor because we were calling a brother to trial, nor because we were content with those who wished to cause the affairs of some to totter, but we held the sessions of the council about the true faith alone.

(11) We confirmed the statements decreed about the faith

[5] That is, Bishop of Constantinople.

by our holy Fathers in the city of Nicaea, and unanimously crowned that great and holy council as setting forth the precisely worded definition of the blameless faith. We confessed together and approved that in no way is it necessary to disturb any of the matters they decreed, but we condemned Nestorius as debasing it and overstepping the boundaries which our holy Fathers set,[6] with the Holy Spirit speaking through them, for thus we have believed.

(12) Greet the brotherhood with you; the brethren with us salute you in the Lord.

[6] Cf. Prv 22.28.

LETTER 93

The second letter of Cyril, to Maximian.[1]

Y BELOVED CLERICS write to me as if your holiness somehow was, perhaps, even vexed that I have not written as to how the affairs of the peace of the holy churches are being composed. I am not so slothful concerning the necessary details of affairs as to wish to be silent and not to explain each of them clearly to those who ought to know these matters and most of all to your holiness. We wrote, therefore, at once and sent the letter through my lord, the most admirable tribune and secretary, Aristolaus.

(2) Yet some men have repeatedly said that all of us and those throughout the East agree only on the profession expounded by our holy and glorious Fathers at Nicaea, disregarding all of the things which we have written against the polluted teachings of Nestorius. Doubtless, somehow, some men have been scandalized at this.

(3) Hence I thought it necessary to inform your holiness through this letter also. Not by disregarding our own writings do we join in praising the profession of the true faith, but we have written them, moving according to the aim of the holy Fathers who have decreed for us the profession of faith. We know that we walk truly upright and are not off the direct path, since we make their words the canon of precision in everything whatsoever.

---

[1] For the critical text of this letter see Schwartz, *ACO* 1.1.7 pp. 162–163. Geerard lists it as number 5393 in *CPG*. Lampe numbers it *ep.* 92 in *PGL*. The place of the letter in the correspondence should be immediately after Letter 49, Cyril to Maximian. That letter deals with the peace between Cyril and John of Antioch, and this letter shows that Maximian was upset about the details of the reconciliation in 433.

(4) Those from the East wrote in the beginning, or rather they made my lord, Acacius, Bishop of Beroea, a man most holy in all things, write that it was pleasing to all of them to unite only on the profession and to set aside the letters and the volumes which we wrote opposing the truth to the innovations of Nestorius. Since I did not smile upon this, I said that, if we suppress our own writings, we condemn our own faith. I neither united with them nor set aside any of my writings, for they were written correctly and with the truth.

(5) But when the most pious Paul, Bishop of Emesa, came to Alexandria saying that all were ready both to anathematize the teachings of Nestorius and to accept his deposition, necessarily the matters concerning communion with them seemed to have been established on these conditions, since in no manner was the profession of the faith being injured by anyone. Moreover, the holy synod which assembled in Ephesus confirmed the profession of the faith again and decreed the deposition of Nestorius, since he was misinterpreting it and twisting around to his own purpose the confession of the faith which had been truly and deliberately set forth by our holy Fathers.

(6) Therefore, let it not be that some men are scandalized because we steadfastly confess that we guard the profession of the faith in which we have also been baptized. Let them know that those, who have believed in the care over his holy churches in moments of crisis on the part of Christ, the Savior of us all, are bearing them out of danger by their most legitimate resolutions against those who do not guard it.

(7) Greet the brotherhood with you. The brethren with us salute you in the Lord.

LETTER 94
(Fragment)[1]

. . . Claudianus, the priest.

(2) For trusting in your holiness indeed as in our brother, because you are able to fulfill all things even those which are difficult, as you know, we are prepared to direct thither a most holy priest with a supply of gifts,[2] trusting, as we said, in him and in your holiness, my lord.

[1] For the critical text of this fragment see Schwartz, *ACO* 1.4 p. 222. He notes that these lines seem to have been excerpted from a letter of Cyril to Maximian, Bishop of Constantinople. Claudianus is the priest mentioned. Geerard numbers this letter 5394 in *CPG*.

[2] The phrase *virtute eulogiarum* is difficult to translate. It appears to be a diplomatic way of saying "a supply of bribes." Claudianus, the priest, seems to have been in charge of them. They were meant to be distributed to persons in the court of the emperor. For the list of them see *ACO* 1.4 pp. 224–225, or Letter 96. The date of the fragment is just after the council in 431.

LETTER 95

To the holy council assembled in this metropolis of Ephesus by the grace of God and a decree of the most God-loving and Christ-loving rulers, Cyril, the Bishop of Alexandria, and Memnon, the [Bishop] of Ephesus.[1]

THE PIOUS DECREE commanded both us and your holinesses[2] to meet in this metropolis of Ephesus so that the true definition of the apostolic faith might be strengthened by our common consent and the heresy which has been instituted by Nestorius might be examined.

(2) But your holy assembly, which is doing all things rightly and canonically, assembled in the holy church[3] in this metropolis and summoned the aforementioned Nestorius, so that he would come to the assembly and offer a defense for the blasphemies he expressed, both in statements and in personal letters, sending forth unholy and sinful utterances against Christ, the Savior of us all, and when he was summoned for the third time and did not choose to come because of being smitten by an evil conscience, [the council] following the laws of the church, has subjected him to deposition, having examined everything about him accurately and having been fully assured that he is both heretical and blasphemous.

(3) When these things had been done and a notice had been made to the wisdom of our most pious and triumphant rulers, John, the Bishop of Antioch, came up to the [city] of Ephesus late, and with difficulty, and when he wished. He gathered, as we learned, certain of those having the ideas of Nestorius,

[1] For the critical text of this letter see Schwartz, *ACO* 1.1.3 pp. 16–17. Geerard numbers this letter 5395 in *CPG*.
[2] The bishops at the council.
[3] June 22, 431 in the Church of Mary, Mother of God.

some of whom were deposed long ago and others who do not have cities but are bishops in name only, as if he was vexed (we do not know how, if the common talk is completely true) that Christ had been glorified because the one uttering blasphemies against him had undergone a just deposition, after he trampled on every ecclesiastical law, outraged all ecclesiastical consequences, and drew up an impious and unlawful document. Thinking he was able to smite us by the pretext of a deposition, he insulted us[4] unbearably, and this although the holy council that deposed Nestorius has over two hundred holy bishops in number. But he has assembled others, heretical and misled, about thirty in number, although they have no authority, either under ecelesiastical laws or by imperial decree, to judge anyone of us or, in truth, to attempt any such thing at all, especially against a more important see. Even if it were possible for him to judge, it was necessary to follow the ecclesiastical canons and to remember to summon us who have been insulted for a defense along with the rest of your entire holy assembly.

(4) But now, having taken none of these into account, nor having put the fear of God in mind, at the very hour in which he entered into the [city] of Ephesus, imperceptibly and with none of us at all knowing the thing which he dared, he has made a mockery of his own person, so that we may not speak of the laws of the church. By a vote of deposition he insults those who knew nothing until today what kind of pretext he would have for this.

(5) Therefore, it follows that we do not thus trample on the laws of the church, nor behave rashly against greater men, nor dare even secretly such things as he did not accomplish, even against one of those who have the lowest rank in the churches who act under his[5] jurisdiction, and is here with those who concurred with him in this.

(6) Necessarily we present to your reverences these documents, swearing by the holy and consubstantial Trinity that John himself has been summoned, together with those who

---

[4]Cyril and Memnon.   [5]Cyril was referring to himself.

have been putting on a play with him, so that, having come to the holy council, they may defend themselves for their own boldness. For we hold ourselves ready to prove him to be unholy and unlawful in causing the attempt of insolence against us.[6]

[6] As a result of this, three bishops were sent to summon John of Antioch to come before the council. One of them, Paul, Bishop of Lampe in Crete, reported afterward to the council that John's house was encircled by soldiers and armed men. The bishops were surrounded, not allowed to approach the door and, although they explained that they had come in peace from the council, they were reviled and had to leave because of a riot that began. See *ACO* 1.1.3 p. 17. The date is during the council in 431. In the sequence of the correspondence this document should come after Letter 24.

LETTER 96

A catalogue of things dispatched from here to the following who are there, by my lord, your most holy brother Cyril.[1]

O PAUL THE PREFECT: four larger wool rugs, two moderate wool rugs, four place covers, four table cloths, six larger *bila* (rugs or curtains), six medium sized *bila*, six stool covers, twelve for doors, two larger caldrons, four ivory chairs, two ivory stools, four *persoina* (= pews?), two larger tables, two ostriches (= pieces of furniture?); and in order that he would help us in the cause about those matters which were written to him: fifty pounds of gold.[2]

(2) And to his domestic, one wool rug, two rugs, four *bila*, two stool covers, and one hundred gold coins.

(3) To Marcella, the chambermaid, the same as was dispatched to him, and that she would persuade Augusta[3] by asking her: fifty pounds of gold.

(4) To Droseria, the chambermaid, the same as was dispatched to Marcella, and that she would help her as was written to her: fifty pounds of gold.

(5) To the prefect Chryseros, that he would cease to oppose us, we were forced to dispatch double amounts: six larger wool rugs, four moderate rugs, four larger rugs, eight place covers, six table cloths, six large *bila* rugs, six medium sized *bila*, six stool covers, twelve for chairs, four larger caldrons, four ivory chairs, four ivory stools, six *persoina*, four larger tables, six ostriches; and if he shall have acted in accordance

---

[1] For the critical text of this letter see Schwartz, *ACO* 1.4 pp. 224–225. Geerard numbers this letter 5396 in *CPG*.

[2] The *libra* was the Roman pound of 12 ounces.

[3] Pulcheria, elder sister of Theodosius II. She received the title Augusta when she became regent in 414.

with what were written to him by the most magnificent Aristolaus with the lord Claudianus intervening as mediator: two
hundred pounds of gold.

(6) And to Solomon, his domestic, two larger wool rugs,
four place covers, four table cloths, four *bila,* four stool covers,
six covers for chairs, six caldrons, two ivory chairs, two ostriches; and just as was written to lord Claudianus, so he may
use persuasion to forward the proposal: fifty pounds of gold.

(7) To lady Heleniana, who is [the wife] of the prefect of the
praetorian guard, the same in all things which were dispatched
to Chryseros, so also to her; and in order that the prefect, persuaded by her, would help us: one hundred pounds of gold. As
to her assessor, Florentinus, just as the things sent to Solomon, equally the same also to him and fifty pounds of gold.

(8) And to the other chamberlains customary suppliant
gifts[4] have been dispatched.

To Romanus the chamberlain: four larger wool rugs, four
place covers, four *bila,* four stool covers, six covers for chairs,
two caldrons, two ivory chairs; and so that he would aid in our
cause: thirty pounds of gold.

(9) To Domninus the chamberlain: four larger wool rugs,
four larger rugs, four medium sized *bila,* four table covers,
four medium sized *bila,* six stool covers, six covers for chairs,
two larger caldrons, two ivory chairs, two ivory stools, four ostriches; and so that he may help us according to those things
which were written to lord Claudianus: fifty pounds of gold.

(10) To Scholasticius, the chamberlain, the same in all things
as those which were dispatched to Chryseros: and one hundred pounds of gold. And to Theodore, his domestic according to the promises of lord Claudianus, if he should persuade
Scholasticius that he desist from friendships with our adversaries: fifty pounds of gold. We have directed also gifts[4] to him

---

[4]The word *eulogiae,* here translated "gifts," appears to be a diplomatic
phrase actually meaning "bribes." It is difficult to pass judgment on this
matter. The court at Constantinople evidently was corrupt. One very revealing item is found on p. 224, line 28: *eulogiae consuetudinariae supplices,* "customary suppliant gifts." If this was customary, the action of Cyril was not so
unusual. How this treasure was transported to the capital is an unanswered
problem. The date of this catalogue was during the time of the council or

which ought to persuade him that he should think in our favor: two wool rugs, two place covers, four table cloths, four rugs, four stools, six stool covers for chairs, two caldrons, two ostriches.

(11) To the most magnificent Artaba the same in all things as those which were dispatched to Scholasticius both in kinds: and that he would help us as was written to him: one hundred pounds of gold.

(12) To Magister, the same in all things as were dispatched to Artaba, in the same kinds: and one hundred pounds of gold. And to his domestic equally in all things as those dispatched to Rufinus.

(13) And to the quaestor, the same as those things which were destined for Magister: and one hundred pounds of gold. And to his domestic Ablalius equally in all things as Eustathius.

(14) A letter was written by your brother to the most reverend clerics so that all these things be dispatched, if anything was done out of devotion to my holy lord and should happen to be accomplished, and that is what is necessary, with the good will and advice of the lord Philip and the lord Claudianus.

---

soon after it. Wickham, *Select Letters*, 66, note 8, translates *persoina* as possibly "pews" or "benches," and suggests that the ostriches must be pieces of furniture or of upholstery. See P. Batiffol, "Les présents de Saint Cyrille à la cour de Constantinople," *Bulletin d'ancienne littérature et d'archéologie chrétienne*, 1 (1911), 247–264 (= *Etudes de Liturgie et d'Archéologie Chrétienne*, Paris, 1919).

LETTER 97
(Fragments)

Of the same Cyril, to the emperor Theodosius.[1]

CCORDINGLY WE confess that the only begotten Son of God is perfect God, consubstantial to the Father according to divinity, and that the same [Son] is consubstantial to us according to humanity. For there was a union of two natures. Wherefore, we confess one Christ, one Son, one Lord.[2]

(2) And, if it seems proper, let us point out as an example the composition in us ourselves according to which we are men. For we are composed of soul and body, and we see two natures, the one of the body and the other of the soul, but one man from both according to a union, and the composition of two natures does not make two men be considered as one, but one man.

(3) For, if we shall give the answer that there is only one Christ from two different natures, those on the opposite side will say, if [he is] entirely one *phusis,* how was he made man or of what kind of flesh was he made?

(4) Those who say that there was a blending, or a mixture, or a confusion of God the Word according to the flesh, these the Catholic and Apostolic Church anathematizes.

[1] For the critical text of this letter see M. Richard, "Deux lettres perdues de Cyrille d'Alexandrie," in *Studia Patristica* 7.1 (= TU 92), ed. F. L. Cross, (Berlin, 1966): 274–275. Geerard numbers this letter 5397 in *CPG*.
[2] Cf. 1 Cor 8.6.

LETTER 98
(Fragment)

Of the same [Cyril], to Photius, a priest of Alexandria.[1]

BUT IF THE TWO natures have been brought into one mingling, because they happen to be of different substances, neither one is preserved, but both have disappeared after they have been blended.

[1] For the critical text of this letter see Richard, "Deux lettres," 275. Geerard numbers this letter 5398 in *CPG*.

LETTER 99
(Fragment)

Of the same [Cyril], from the [letter] to the monks of Constanti-nople.[1]

E DO NOT SAY that the Father of the flesh[2] is the one in heaven[3] nor, on the other hand, in turn, that the nature of divinity was born from a woman.

[1] For the critical text of this letter see Schwartz, *Codex vaticanus gr. 1431*, p. 34. After this brief fragment he comments that "the letter appears to be lost." Geerard numbers this letter 5399 in *CPG*.

[2] That is, the body of Christ.

[3] That is, God the Father. Mary, Mother of God, conceived of the Holy Spirit. See Lk 1.35.

LETTER 100

THE FIRST LETTER WHICH SAINT CYRIL, THE BISHOP, SENT TO THE MONASTIC BRETHREN ON THE FAITH OF THE CHURCH

Greetings in our Lord from Cyril to the fathers and brethren, our fellow ministers, holders of the apostles' faith, blessed and reverend monks.[1]

I AM CONVINCED OF your excellencies' steadfast mind which refuses to waver this way and that for it is secured firmly in itself. I declare that the fruit of a God-loving mind is this: that a man should not give too ready heed to various people's utterances nor be disposed too indiscriminately and hastily to condemn his Christian brethren to whose constancy he has had long, previous testimony. Much experience of them will have shown that they adhere to the faith of their fathers because they are friends of truth. In such as these I pray that I also may be numbered.

(2) For I adhere to the faith of the sainted Fathers who assembled at Nicaea in all my discourses. No other path do I know but the orthodox faith, for I was nurtured, as were your holinesses, in the faith of the Gospel and the words of the

---

[1] This letter is preserved in Syriac. It was published by R. Y. Ebied and L. R. Wickham, "An Unknown Letter of Cyril of Alexandria in Syriac," in *The Journal of Theological Studies*, n.s. 22(1971): 420–434. At the end of the article an English translation is presented, which is here reprinted by permission of the editors of *The Journal of Theological Studies* (Oxford University Press). The authors suggest that the date is about 432. The letter is addressed to the monks at Constantinople. It may be a forgery, or it may be a letter which is not otherwise preserved. The personal references by Cyril about himself are similar to those found in his Letter 33, to Acacius of Beroea. Geerard numbers this letter 5400 in *CPG*.

apostles. It is this faith which I shall do my best to teach the churches. But seeing that certain persons, whether because they have failed to understand my words or, with some ground unknown to me who say nothing difficult,[2] have cast aspersions on me as a heretic, stirring up, it may be, many of your neighbors, I have seen fit to say a few words and declare my mind.

(3) I have never been of Apollinaris' persuasion (God forbid!) nor ever shall be. It is not my assertion that the holy body, which God the Word put on, lacked a soul. No, it contained a rational soul. Nor have I ever asserted or declared, as many report against us, mixture, confusion, or intermingling of natures—folly to think and folly to utter! I have never said that God the Word's nature is passible, nor been inclined to the doctrine of Arius; up till now God has not groaned over me (i.e., on that score). For how could I have been of this persuasion, one who so many times in the presence of the whole church has refuted and execrated Arius' teachings? Your holinesses will believe that I am not the kind of man who has repented of his former views.

(4) I now come to the point of writing down or stating these matters. Of old, indeed from the very first, I have, by our Lord's grace, been in the orthodox and immaculate faith. The letter written by me to Nestorius, while he was at Constantinople and prior to the assembling of the holy synod at Ephesus, need be sent.[3] So when your excellencies receive this letter, I trust that it will silence the tongues of those who dare to pretend otherwise. For in those chapters,[4] which I set down, I anathematized Nestorius' opinion, after having gathered from his writings the blasphemies affirmed by him. That what I say is so, the letter written and placed before the chapters [lit. above the chapters] bears witness, a letter wherein the true

[2] Ebied and Wickham note: "So the Syriac, but perhaps representing rather 'because they have failed to understand my words, (I do not know how, because I say nothing difficult)'."
[3] Letter 17 of Cyril, at the end of which are the famous twelve anathemas.
[4] The anathemas at the end of Letter 17.

faith is expounded in writing. But since I hear that some people are alleging that, as they put it, "after he had changed his views he wrote the letter and put at the head of it [lit. above] the chapters", let me say that this is not so. After the letter had been written we added and connected the chapters to it, anathematizing in them Nestorius' teaching, and those who adhere to it.

(5) Greet all the brotherhood. All the brethren who are with me greet you.

LETTER 101

The Holy Cyril: The Sixth Discourse of the Glaphuda *(sic)*[1]

THE DIVINE Law says, "If there is found in one of your cities, which the Lord your God is giving you, a man or a woman who has committed evil before the Lord your God by transgressing his commandment, bring out that man or woman to the gate of the city, and stone them (sic) with stones so that they die. On the testimony of two or three witnesses the one who is to die shall be put to death."[2]

(2) For in that time, when men used to trample and do evil against the worship of God, it was of no benefit for a man to be compassionate. For it was right in that time that a man who turned from the worship of God should be rejected and despised by those who did worship God. It was the law of retribution, by which one was bound with respect to one who

[1] This is a translation of a Syriac text published by I. Guidi in *Atti della R. Accademia dei Lincei*, Ser. 4, rendiconti 2 (Rome, 1886): 545–47. *Glaphuda* should read *Glaphyra*, a work by Cyril of Alexandria, an exposition of select passages of the Pentateuch. The first two paragraphs of this text have nothing to do with the rest. Geerard lists it in *CPG* 5401 as a letter to Rabbula of Edessa. This is the first time that it has been translated into English. Thanks are due to Mr. Edward Mathews of the Department of Semitics at The Catholic University of America who translated it from Syriac into English. The part of the text which contains the letter presents a problem because of the use of the word "commingling" once and "mingled" twice. During the Nestorian controversy Cyril rejected any terminology except "union" when speaking of the Incarnation and the union of Christ's divinity and humanity. This is clear from Letters 11(a), 17, 40 and 55. In Letter 40 he maintained an ineffable and unconfused union. In Letter 98 the noun *mixis*, "a mingling," is rejected. However, the translator into Syriac may have had before him a genuine letter of Cyril and used the word in these three instances innocently as the equivalent of the Greek text. If it was deliberate, since this became a Monophysite term after Cyril's death, he was giving the letter a tinge of their diction and meaning. Geerard numbers this letter 5401 in *CPG*.
[2] Cf. Dt 17.2, 5, and 6.

erred, that he should put far from him the natural power of love and every type of clemency and with perfect severity of the worship of God he should perform that which is pleasing to God.[3]

(3) The things of his humanity are to be placed with his divinity because of his commingling[4] according to that which is written in the first letter to the Corinthians, "If they had known, they would not have crucified the Lord of glory."[5] For it was not a heavenly man who came down from heaven but rather God who was mingled[6] with man. And the Lord of glory, who was God, could not be crucified unless he received a body. For this reason after the command was given by our Lord to the apostles that they baptize in the name of the Father, Son and Holy Spirit,[7] the blessed apostle Peter in the Acts [of the Apostles] said to those who came to believe "Repent and be baptized in the name of the Lord Jesus Christ,"[8] so that he might make manifest that the name of our Lord Jesus Christ thus gives life and saves those who are baptized in it, according to the holy names of the Father, Son and Holy Spirit.

(4) The blessed Apostle Paul also teaches us that our Lord Jesus Christ, who was born of Mary, is the true Son of God, saying in the letter to Titus that "we are waiting for the appearance of the great God and our life-giver Jesus Christ."[9] And he also says concerning the Jews in the letter to the Romans, "from them there appeared the Messiah in the flesh who is God over all, to whom be glory and blessings forever. Amen."[10]

(5) And also when our Lord asked his disciples, "Who do men say that I, the Son of Man, am?"[11] Simon Cephas said to him, "You are Christ, the Son of the living God."[12] And because of this he called him blessed, for flesh and blood did not

---

[3] Here the first part of the Syriac text ends.
[4] See note 1.   [5] 1 Cor 2.8.
[6] See note 1.   [7] Cf. Mt 28.19.
[8] Acts 2.38.   [9] Cf. Ti 2.13.
[10] Cf. Rom 9.5.   [11] Cf. Mt 16.13.
[12] Mt 16.16

reveal it to him, but the Father who is in heaven.[13] And Isaiah also says, "A child is born to us, a son is given to us and his name will be called Wonderful, Counselor, and Mighty God."[14] Isaiah also says, "Behold, a virgin will conceive and bear a son and his name will be called Emmanuel, which is God with us."[15] And many other testimonies such as these do lovers of the truth find in the Holy Scriptures.

(6) For the creed which was written down by the Fathers at Nicaea also teaches us that the Lord Jesus Christ is one, who before the ages was begotten of the glorious nature of the Father, while in later times he took flesh and became man from the Blessed Virgin Mary for our sake and for our salvation. That same one suffered and rose, and in the suffering of his person bore our sufferings. For our Savior is not a man, nor do we declare that he is separate from his divinity as the deceitful division of those for whom it is right that they be separated, because they stir up the Church of God and disturb the simplicity of her faith with the perversity of their words.

(7) We, however, knowing that the Son of God is one, do not separate his divinity from his humanity by his human sufferings, nor because of his divine actions do we estrange his divinity from his humanity. That same one is perfect God and perfect man. He is Son of God and also Son of Man, without mother in heaven and without father on earth, who, as a man, hungered, was tired, and slept, and as God worked wonders and gave life to the dead.

(8) Even the body of the Son of God, which he took from human nature, we hold to be life-giving, because it was mingled[16] with the living God according to the word of our Lord which he spoke in the Gospel, "Unless you eat my body and drink my blood, you do not have eternal life."[17] For if, as those blasphemers say, our Lord's body is not beneficial because it was taken from human nature, then according to their expression neither is the living mystery[18] which is the

[13] Cf. Mt 16.17
[14] Is 9.6.
[15] Is 7.14 and Mt 1.23.
[16] See note 1.
[17] Cf. Jn 6.53.
[18] The Sacred Host in the Holy Eucharist.

outward sign of his body able to be of any aid to those who receive it.

(9) These things about which I have written for the love of God which is within you transcend the scope of a letter, but I am writing from the suffering of my soul and from the great love which I have for your holiness. Great exertion is a small effort for us, since we are contending for the true faith for which the blood of the holy Fathers was shed.

LETTER 102
(Fragments)[1]

For in a letter to John, Bishop of Antioch, whose beginning is:

My most religious lord, the Bishop of Beronicia, sent a letter to me which had been sent by your holiness, Cyril, written in this manner:

OR SOME HOLY monks from Antioch came to me and indicated that some of the most religious bishops of Phoenicia were uttering in the churches stupid words which introduced in them the mark of the madness of Nestorius. However, I advised them that, as long as the suspected ones anathematized Nestorius and the teachings of Nestorius, and did not think otherwise, it rather would be enough for them.

[And, after other words:]

(2) Let it come to pass that peace should prevail for those who have anathematized the teachings of Nestorius or his unclean words, and for those not now saying any such thing in church, lest some be scandalized. But indeed it is clear also to your holiness what great insanity it is that they anathematize these even in writing but still think and say them not only to those who are subject to them, the congregations and the cler-

---

[1] These fragments were preserved in Syriac and were translated into Latin in Joseph Lebon, *Severi Antiocheni liber contra impium Grammaticum. Orationis tertiae pars prior,* CSCO 94 (Louvain, 1952): 142. From the contents these fragments should be dated as after the reconciliation in 433. Geerard numbers this letter 5402 in *CPG.*

ics, but also to others from different states who are found in
the sacred assemblies.

(3) Let your holiness, therefore, deign to remove the cause
of scandal and by a general letter admonish all the most religious bishops who are subject to you.

LETTER 103
(Fragment)

In another letter whose beginning is:[1]

Happy indeed to all men [is] peace,

he [Cyril] wrote these words to him:[2]

LONGINUS THE MAGNIFICENT count, and his most honored wife have written to me that the churches of Isauria[3] are disturbed because the most religious bishops and clerics who are in it dare without fear in the congregations to express the opinions of Nestorius and to make his idle talk public.

---

[1] This fragment of a letter was preserved in Syriac and translated into Latin in Lebon, *Severi Antiocheni,* 142. Geerard numbers this letter 5403 in *CPG.*
[2] John of Antioch.
[3] An inland district in south central Asia Minor north of Cilicia.

LETTER 104[1]
(Fragments)

And again in a letter to him[2] that begins:

As a gift of Christian love I just received the written words of your holiness,

Cyril wrote thus:

OR THOSE ARRIVING not only from many different bishops but also from monks bring letters and all, as if in one voice, accuse the holy bishops of Cilicia because they not only depart from the peace which came to be for the holy churches with the help of Christ, but they also expel from the community, and dishonor by excommunications, priests, deacons and archimandrites when they utter any word in favor of faith in Christ.

(2) However, I have not ceased to advise those arriving that they should be silent and rather hold firm, and least of all require that in a very short time the disturbance should be settled which has been aroused in the churches, and they should rather await the restoration of affairs proceeding bit by bit, which they say will be by the help of God and is not far away.

---

[1] These fragments were preserved in Syriac and translated into Latin in Lebon, *Severi Antiocheni*, 142–143. From the contents the fragment should be dated as about the time of the reconciliation in 433. Geerard numbers this letter 5404 in *CPG*.

[2] John of Antioch.

LETTER 105[1]
(Fragment)

And to Dalmatius, a priest and abbot, staying in the capital city[2] in a letter whose beginning is:

My holy and most religious lord John, Bishop of Antioch,

Cyril wrote about the matter thus:

OWEVER, WHEN those who have been snatched away by the madness of Nestorius have been instructed bit by bit, they will hasten to that which is right. But if anyone fights against them, they will remain in those [errors] for the most part in which they are involved.

---

[1] This fragment was preserved in Syriac and was translated into Latin in Lebon, *Severi Antiocheni,* 143. From the contents the fragment should be dated as about the time of the reconciliation in 433. Geerard numbers this letter 5405 in *CPG.*

[2] Constantinople.

LETTER 106[1]
(Fragment)

. . . so that we travel abroad from Alexandria to Ephesus. Set aside all immediate affairs which concern your holiness, for God will direct them. And there is nothing in his sight which compares with what concerns the faith. I pray that things are going well for you in the Lord, beloved [brother] whom I honor.

[1] Only the ending of the letter is extant. It was addressed to Victor, a monk of Egypt. Preserved in Coptic and edited with a French translation by U. Bouriant, *Fragments coptes relatifs au concile d'Éphèse*, Mémoires publiés par les membres de la mission archéologique française au Caire, vol. 8 (Paris, 1892): 5. It was also translated into German by Wilhelm Kraatz, *Koptische Akten zum ephesinischen Konzil vom Jahre 431*, TU 11.2 (Leipzig, 1904): 4. The translation of this letter is based on Kraatz's German translation. The fragment is to be dated according to the contents as just before the council in 431. Geerard numbers this letter 5406 in *CPG*.

LETTER 107

A copy of the memorandum which was given to the God-loving monk, abbot Victor, by the holy archbishop Cyril.[1]

F GOD WILLS IT, after the holy feast[2] we will hasten to set forth from Alexandria to Ephesus. But your piety which outstrips us might in the meantime be on guard at other places, since, as I think, some wish to wrong us, or rather some of the bishops, and their clerics who are with us, wish to bring petitions before the pious emperor so that they would be heard at the council, or rather, the great prefect [would be heard] by the throne or by the governor of the province. In brief, all these ponder within themselves how to disturb the purpose of the council.

(2) Therefore, watch and take care so that, if it comes to pass in this manner, you admonish them that the teaching of the faith should remain steadfast above all, and afterwards that, if they wish to denounce a bishop or cleric, they may hear a judgment at the council or in Constantinople. For we do not wish to be heard by the governors at Ephesus, or above all by an Asiatic court of justice, lest we be oppressed by many difficulties in a foreign country.

(3) But ask also in regard to this matter that no one except one of the zealous orthodox be sent to Ephesus, who has the support of the governors in that place, so that he watch over the good order of the city and arrange us safely without harm

---

[1] The translation of this letter is based upon Kraatz, *Koptische Akten*, 5–6. For the critical text with French translation see Bouriant, *Fragments coptes*, 6–8. Victor was going to Constantinople with instructions from Cyril as to what he should do there. Afterwards he returned to his monastery in Egypt, cf. Kraatz, *Koptische Akten*, 5. Geerard numbers this letter 5407 in *CPG*.

[2] Easter 431.

as strangers and, moreover, protect the council so that no one may do it any violence.

(4) If Nestorius asks about count Irenaeus, whom he has made one of the illustrious, suffer it not at all that that one come alone to Ephesus, since he belongs to his faction[3] and will busy himself to please him, and cares not for us in any way, and also does not requite the abusive treatment which will fall to our lot through some people, but continues moreover to protect only Nestorius and to fight for him.

(5) This is indeed now necessary: either Lausus should be sent alone, or again he should come with Irenaeus. We are strangers and fear very much lest some stir up the people to rise against us, or again that the monks who are in that place drive the council asunder so that we are not able to assemble and as a result that we flee all at once. For that fellow Nestorius will use many intrigues. Indeed he comes to Ephesus according to the imperial command, but if he pursues us by his intrigues, he will denounce us as if we had departed of our own accord, and will contrive riots and tumults against us.

[3] The faction in Constantinople favoring Nestorius.

LETTER 108

[Cyril, to] the bishops [Komarius and Potamon] and to Victor, father of monks, beloved in the Lord, whom I honor, greetings.[1]

OLLOWING AT ALL times the commands of the pious God-loving emperor we went forth from Alexandria, I and the devout bishops with me, and many of them came to Ephesus. But our ship had to endure ill winds and only with difficulty were we able to arrive at Lycia, since at that place God disposed our landing. We traveled along an island and came to Ephesus on the Sabbath, one day before the holy feast of Pentecost. There indeed our ship could not go into the harbor. Because there are landing places in it,[2] I went on board a small skiff, I and the clerics who were with me, and I went into the city.

(2) And so the multitude of citizens received me with much joy, since they are good Christians. And at once they escorted me into the church. And when I had finished the prayer, I went into the lodging which they had prepared for me. But on this same day there came the one[3] who had stirred up controversies against himself alone and the true faith, and no riot or disorder took place on our[4] arrival.

(3) And as it came to be evening on that day, Nestorius sent two of the God-fearing bishops to us and said, "Come, in

---

[1] The translation of this letter is based upon Kraatz, *Koptische Akten,* 11–13. For the critical text with French translation see Bouriant, *Fragments coptes,* 12–16. Cyril addressed Letter 23 to Komarius and Potamon. Geerard numbers this letter 5408 in *CPG. CPG* 5409 is addressed to them also and Victor is called "father of the monks" there. The date is 431.

[2] Kraatz noted that the Coptic of this clause is faulty.

[3] Nestorius.

[4] Kraatz noted that the Coptic text should read "on his arrival."

order that we may carry out the service [5] which is customary at the time of lamp lighting." There were with us many bishops, foreign and Egyptian, and also my lord and father the devout Flavian, who all at once unanimously cried out, "This, namely, simply to associate at a service, is not proper, but what is proper is that we above all decide the subject on account of which the council has assembled and that we determine the formula to which it is necessary that those who please God hold fast in the future." Since then some said that it is proper that the council carry out the service and that we should meanwhile put up with Nestorius and not dispute with him until the coming formula has once unanimously been established; thus we deliberated with one another that, if we did anything of such a kind, those who adhered to his holiness [6] would stir up riots against us and many disorders; therefore, we kept ourselves altogether apart from the service unanimously, as it were.

(4) But we said to the God-fearing and devout bishop Memnon,[7] "You alone are worthy to carry out the service." But he feared a great deal lest he go and carry out the service while the council was apart from him, and lest that one [8] might enter with trickery, since he had sought to do this at the hour of day for lamp lighting. On that account he commanded his clerics that they alone go and stop the service.

(5) Since, now, I indeed know that some have written to Constantinople about my character, that I have brought with me from Alexandria a crowd of reckless fellows, and ships loaded with grain, and they have brought forward many other slanders against me, for this reason it was necessary for me to inform your piety also about this matter, to the effect that neither has any reckless fellow at all followed me nor have we brought a single measure of grain, but God is my witness that

---

[5] Kraatz in the text has the Greek word σύναξις, "meeting" and in parentheses translated it as *Abendmahl*, "evening meal." There are overtones of a liturgical service here.

[6] Nestorius.

[7] Bishop of Ephesus.

[8] Nestorius.

we have been given in Ephesus small amounts of money for the bakeries by which they supply us daily the ration of bread, for we are here each isolated with only two attendants and the necessary clerics who attend us in a fitting manner.

(6) Since now the devout bishops have not yet come to Ephesus, neither the Bishop of Antioch nor the Bishop of Jerusalem, we are not able up to now to do anything at all. Most especially the devout bishops who have assembled became very dejected because they wish to settle the matter speedily. But I answered them in this manner, "Since the bishops were allowed to depart from their provinces and all are on their way, it is just that we still wait for one another. Therefore, now indeed do not give to those who are slanderous in words the opportunity to write any other such thing instead. For we have a goal of such a kind that we fight in all array and peace[9] for the truth and strive in a way that is proper for those to see who wage war against the glory of the faith of Christ our Savior in an outrageous way."

(7) I pray that things are going well for you in the Lord, my beloved [brethren,] whom I love.

[9] Kraatz noted that the meaning of the Coptic word used here is uncertain.

LETTER 109

Cyril, to the bishops Komarius and Potamon and to Victor, father of the monks, his beloved [brethren] whom he loves in the Lord, greetings.[1]

LERICS OF THE Church of Constantinople arrived in Ephesus before us, who outstripped us in bringing great accusations against Nestorius, that he was debasing the faith which our holy Fathers and the divinely inspired Scripture have given us. They were very afraid, however, since they knew that someone had been sent from the palace[2] to pursue them from the city in order to convey them bound to Constantinople.

(2) But the council stands in great need of men of this kind, not in order that we might bring forward [properly: uncover[3]] accusations against him, but in order that we may search rather in truth after a matter of faith. Indeed let it be urged at the present time that nothing of that kind should happen, so that no obstacle may arise to the establishment of the holy doctrine, when one pursues those capable of convicting him,[4] in case he should deny it.

(3) I pray that things are going well for you in the Lord, my beloved [brethren,] whom I love.

---

[1] The translation of this letter is based upon Kraatz, *Koptische Akten*, 24–25. For the critical text with French translation see Bouriant, *Fragments coptes*, 28–29. Geerard numbers this letter 5409 in *CPG*. The date of the letter is 431.

[2] In Constantinople.

[3] Kraatz inserted this note in the text.

[4] Nestorius.

LETTER 110
(Fragments)

Three letters of Cyril, the Archbishop of Alexandria, to Sinuthius.[1]

. . . in order to greet your reverence[2] through Didymus, the prudent lector, he who was appointed to disseminate the writings worthy of the pious ones, the bishops of the metropolitan province. This, then, we are now doing. . . . [approximately four lines missing] Tell me then, for the love of God, everything which would cause me joy. May your reverence continue to enjoy good health, and to instruct by means of the monastic contest according to the custom which appears to be of benefit to the monks who are under your care.

HERE IS A BIG rumor, and it has been communicated to me through the clergy who are in Constantinople, that the pious and Christ-loving emperor has decided to send someone from among those who are very close to him to urge you and me to come to him.[3] And, so it seems, we shall not find a way to avoid the invitation. So I wish now that your reverence would come to Alexandria and do so quickly in case it is necessary for us to embark together. But meanwhile do

[1] The three letters were translated by Reverend D. W. Johnson, S. J., from Coptic into English for this volume. For the Coptic text see J. Leipoldt, *Sinutii archimandritae vita et opera omnia*, CSCO 42, *Scriptores Coptici*, ser. 2, t. 4 (Paris, 1908): 225–226. Geerard numbers this letter 5410 in *CPG*. From the context of the letters the date would be soon after Letter 1 of Cyril to the monks in Egypt. Judging from what is said the letters should be considered genuine.

[2] Sinuthius or Shenute was archimandrite of monks in Egypt.

[3] There is no evidence in the rest of Cyril's correspondence that this invitation from the emperor was ever issued or that the journey to Constantinople was ever necessary.

not let this get to outsiders. Rather let it be known to you alone. Make haste to come.

THE LETTER OF your reverence was given to me who is not uninformed about your zeal. For it is not sloth which checks your path toward us, but physical illness and suffering concealed in your entrails and your ribs. Now, when I realized this, I was filled with great sadness. In any case, I pray that you be released from what has befallen you and regain health in soul and body, while progressing as usual and guiding the monks who are under your care in everything pleasing to God. And, as for us, we too are healed by your prayers. It is possible too for your love to bring this about, both that you might come to us and that you might enjoy our solicitude according to the good custom.

APPENDICES

APPENDIX 1

A letter of Sixtus to the most holy archbishop, Cyril.[1]

 WAS DELIGHTED at what was revealed to me through the letter from your holiness concerning my holy fellow bishops whom a short acquaintance and a happy event have shown of what kind and of what a number they are. And perhaps we would trust less in letters about them, if otherwise the presence of the men testifying to it prevailed over the testimony from them. We truly have known bishops of the Lord, and we have known men full of spiritual love, which first of all is given by God himself, and the judgment of God concerning us has shown them still more affectionate.

(2) For our election[2] kept them present and since they themselves were honoring a bishop in all the things accomplished, they indicated to us the presence itself of your holiness, which, not without great deserving, we always embrace in brotherly fashion. For the universal church owes you so much that all are under your control, you who have conquered all men everywhere.

(3) Accordingly, since our son, Themison, the archdeacon, is taking care of it and suggests everything wisely, we have given to him the proper letter to our brothers and fellow bishops for whom our fellow bishops, mentioned above, requested a letter. For those letters were sufficient which I sent before

---

[1] For the critical text of this papal letter to Cyril see Schwartz, *ACO* 1.1.7 pp. 143–144. The letter is added to the correspondence by the translator. It is not reckoned as part of the collection by Geerard in *CPG*, or by Lampe in *PGL*. The importance of the letter is that it contains the decision and definition of the new Pope, Sixtus, regarding John of Antioch and his adherents. The date of the letter would be before the reconciliation of 433 and just after summer of 432.

[2] Sixtus was elected to the Roman Papacy on July 31, 432.

this through the clerics of the Church of Constantinople and later through the deacons of your holiness, which letters were full of the necessary details. And now following the recollection of your fraternal concern and our own character I have not omitted what was wisely suggested to me, confessing my thanks and placing among my benefits this which I have been persuaded was bestowed on me by heaven, so that we might exchange with your unanimity these very words concerning my election and concerning the faith.

(4) Both in regard to the Bishop of Antioch[3] and whoever of the rest with him who have chosen to be followers of Nestorius, and in regard to all those directing the churches according to their ecclesiastical wisdom, having reached this conclusion, we define that there must be watchfulness in order that, if they should recover sobriety of mind and with their own leader should condemn all that the holy council condemned, since we are confirming it, they may ascend to the assembly of the bishops. For just as by abiding by their previous actions they were not able to be in our communion, so we desire that they be welcomed, when they remove the charge against them through the unity and peace of the churches, as we have said. But they will be found to have carried out the same sentence upon themselves, if by remaining outside they should show themselves comrades and accomplices with the one who has been overthrown and thrust out for such impiety.

[3] John of Antioch.

APPENDIX 2

A proposal made by Acacius, Bishop of Beroea, by John, Bishop of Antioch, and those with him, and sent from him to the blessed Cyril through Aristolaus.[1]

E ABIDE BY THE faith of the holy Fathers who assembled at Nicaea, which has the evangelical and apostolic teaching and does not need addition. The most holy and most blessed Athanasius, the Bishop of Alexandria and confessor, in the letter to the most blessed and most God-loving Epictetus, the Bishop of Corinth, makes its thought clear.

(2) We accordingly abide by it as having the precise interpretation of the faith mentioned before. We reject all the doctrines introduced recently either through letters or through pamphlets as confusing the common people, since we are content with the ancient legislation of the Fathers, and obey the one who said, "Remove not the ancient landmarks which your Fathers set up."[2]

---

[1] For the critical text of this letter see Schwartz, *ACO* 1.1.7 p. 146. The letter is not in Migne. It is added to the collection by the translator since it is addressed to Cyril. It is not reckoned among Cyril's Letters by Geerard in *CPG*, or by Lampe in *PGL*. The contents are important for they show the reaction of Acacius of Beroea to Cyril's Letter 92, and consequently the proposal should be dated before the reconciliation in 433.

[2] Prv 22.28.

APPENDIX 3

A letter of John, Bishop of Antioch, to Cyril, Archbishop of Alexandria, sent through Paul of Emesa and not accepted by Cyril, concerning the agreement.[1]

UR SAVIOR AND LORD, Jesus Christ, handed on to his disciples countless saving instructions, as well as these two which seem to be diametrically opposite to each other, but preserve all harmony toward each other, I mean peace and war, war, on the one hand, for his sake and for the sake of the pious confession in him, and peace, on the other hand, from him to his own.

(2) According to this the union of the faithful everywhere on earth is established, since there is known to be one church of those who preserve his holy purpose among the pagans and the foreigners everywhere in the world. But there is necessity rather of his all-holy words in which he both imposes the war and grants his peace to us, for he says, "I did not come to send peace upon the earth but a sword"[2] and "My peace I give unto you."[3] When, therefore, the pious confession in Christ is in a struggle, then the war is better and he knows how to save those engaged, for they are defending, not their own, but the Lord's interests. But when the pious faith in him is vigorous, then the peace of those who agree is healthy in the whole ecclesiastical body. These words have not been simply said by me, nor in order that I might hold a discussion, for this is far from my character.

[1] For the critical text of this letter see Schwartz, *ACO* 1.1.7 pp. 151–152. It is not listed as part of Cyril's correspondence by Geerard in *CPG*, or by Lampe in *PGL*. It was added to the collection by the translator for the contents show the attitude of John of Antioch at the time of the reconciliation in 433.

[2] Cf. Mt 10.34.   [3] Jn 14.27.

(3) I desire to show that the disagreement with you, most
God-loving brother, happened in a crisis of truth, not because
of something physical, nor because of hatred or supposed
smallness of soul. We had a certain disposition and arrangement toward each other even more than those before us. A
happy meeting face to face did not nurture this but a series of
letters welded it together, the fairest and strongest possible.
Our disagreement had as its cause the sending of those documents, and it would be an advantage if it had not happened.
It is necessary that your reverence believe me how much it
alienated us, so that we did not think they were yours in the
beginning. Especially your holiness truly knows this from our
letters written to certain persons. But they seemed to be by
one who did not think with us, that is, not with the church.
And I entertained this thought at once, totally disquieted
at them.

(4) No small remedy for these documents has come about,
and the recent letter from you,[4] most God-fearing brother,
furnishes even more hope to us of the perfect cure. That
letter was sent to my lord, the most God-fearing Acacius, our
common father, and it gladdened all who are lovers of ecclesiastical peace. With them we also were wonderfully pleased,
even if it was joined with many brotherly charges concerning
us. It furnished to us a certain conviction, not a small one, and
does not need much addition. You said this, which you yourself promised to do, that, when peace comes to be, what are
matters of conviction will be clarified even further.[5] And this
also delighted us when we learned that you accepted with exceeding joy the letter of the blessed Athanasius, our common
father,[6] as being sufficient to settle the controversies for all,
not only by its being correct, but also from his trustworthiness
by cancelling the conflict. Let him be for us a sufficient inter-
preter of the faith set forth by the holy Fathers at Nicaea, because there are some men of those both in the church and of
those outside the church who propose it as bringing some

---

[4] John had seen Letter 33 addressed to Acacius of Beroea.
[5] See Letter 33.
[6] John referred to this in the proposal which Cyril rejected. See Appendix 2.

great help to men, but they pervert some things in it to their own thought and to what simply presents itself to the mind of each. It is enough to say that much.

(5) Accordingly, since these matters are well at rest, let the things, which were the cause of the difference which arose between us, hereafter cease. Let what is of peace prevail, since the people all over the world are suffering because of the different opinions and are dragged about hither and thither. Many people do not know those dragging them about nor do the people know what they are saying or affirming about certain subjects. The snowstorms of excommunications are going beyond bounds everywhere and intended revilings abound of brothers against brothers, bishops against bishops, people against people.

(6) Some call the Christians Jews as abuse, and there is the ancient reviling of Apollinaris itself also against the universal church, which the common people have taken up with arrogance, for that impious man and enemy of God called[7] those who were arrayed against his own error, I mean the Fathers of the church, Jews and was not ashamed. And the others address these, who were often in communion with them in the ineffable mysteries, as pagans and worse than pagans. There is nothing else to see happening everywhere in the world except disorder, unheralded war, unrestrained wrath, and savagery exceeding all barbaric inhumanity, and there is no one suffering "by the collapse of Joseph."[8] We bite and we devour one another, and then we have been destroyed by one another, providing pleasure to the enemies of piety.

(7) I say this not accusing some and discharging others from blame but writing against the confusion which has happened through our common failures. Since the Gospel is advancing and the pagans and heretics are becoming fewer, necessarily the enemies of piety bear ill-will against us, and by

[7] John used the historical present in the Greek throughout.
[8] Am 6.6. The northern kingdom in Israel was referred to as Joseph, because he was the ancestor of the tribes of Ephraim and Manasseh. See P. J. King, *JBC* 14:17, 20. John of Antioch here applies the words of Amos to his situation and that of the bishops of the East.

grasping the opportunity of the present tumult fearlessly ruin everything. Hence suddenly the holy things of Christianity are trampled on, and quickly "the enemies of God raise a tumult, and lift up their heads" and "against his people they plot craftily."[9]

(8) For all these reasons I and my lord, the most holy bishop Acacius, exhorted my brother, an admirer of your reverence, my lord, the most holy bishop Paul, and he himself grasped the chance to go quickly to your holiness. He is a man always esteemed among ecclesiastics, one who had well known how to conduct affairs even nobly, and who possesses reverence toward God. Using these talents he has often brought many things together for the common good, leading the way under God, and even more he brings them together through the innate earnestness which is present in him.

(9) Deign to see him gladly and have confidence in him as if in me and be assured by him as by me, and consider with him whatever can set the world straight again. Let the discussion with your piety not be so much either of me or of yourself but of how, after the scandals have been taken away, it is proper that the Church of Christ return more quickly to herself, in order that, when these things have occurred, what has been recommended to the most reverend and Christ-loving emperor concerning ecclesiastical peace may succeed.

[9] Cf. Ps 82(83). 3, 4.

APPENDIX 4

It says: The letter of Epiphanius, archdeacon and companion of Cyril, to Maximian, Bishop of Constantinople, in which the effort of Cyril and of those who are with him is further demonstrated.[1]

To my most holy lord and most God-loving bishop, father of fathers and archbishop, Maximian, your Epiphanius [sends greetings].

HE THINGS WHICH rather often have been written to us by your holiness were not so full of disorder as the things which now have been sent to my lord Cyril, most holy in all things, the brother of your holiness, which made him all the more fall into a recurrence of illness, and to the most admirable tribune, Aristolaus, and which were directed to my humility. And with your pardon I refer to the petitions of both of them, not only as to the things which once were done but also as to the things which now have been decided anew, and at which your most holy and God-loving brother, Cyril, has been saddened and likewise the most famous tribune, Aristolaus.

(2) For while previously the [bishops] of the East sought that the documents[2] which your most holy brother, Cyril, proposed, these he himself by anathematizing (should cast aside),[3] that is, he should place (himself) outside the Catholic Church,

---

[1] For the critical text of this letter see Schwartz, *ACO* 1.4 pp. 222–224, number 293. It is the introduction to the *Breve* or catalogue of treasures which were sent by Cyril to members of the court at Constantinople as bribes. The evident purpose was to obtain a decree by the emperor, Theodosius II, against Nestorius. The letter and its accompanying catalogue show clearly how corrupt the court was. This apparently was the way to be effective there and obtain results. The writer was with Cyril during an illness, and the letter is quite blunt, even too frank, in a situation where Cyril might have been more diplomatic.

[2] Cyril's proposals at the Council of Ephesus.

[3] Schwartz emended a lacuna with *abiceret* and *se*.

in this matter my lord, my most holy father Cyril fought back and kept saying what the holy and great council said, recognizing by whose power it decreed, that they are of the right and true faith and it subjected John,[4] with the rest, to excommunication. "And how," he said, "shall I make peace with them and overthrow a conciliar judgment?" Moreover, the most admirable tribune, Aristolaus, urged on him that he should carry out things divinely sanctioned. And my lord Cyril, most holy in all things, of necessity ordered that, since an anathema had been imposed, his holiness[5] should say that he proposed these very things, not according to a heretical meaning, but whatever even seems reprehensible has been said with zeal and ardor towards our Lord, Jesus Christ, who was denied[6] by Nestorius, and moreover that all [the bishops] of the East anathematize Nestorius and his teaching, and that thus they would be received for the purpose of peace.

(3) However, when the most magnificent Aristolaus commanded those who were with John and lord Acacius,[7] because lord Acacius ought to urge John, they sent Paul, evading this, so that nothing about him[8] would be kept in memory but he should be at rest. Therefore, since my lord, my most holy father Cyril was held back by a severe illness, it seemed best that those matters be deferred. However, after some days Paul the bishop showed to the most magnificent tribune a letter of the most impious John to the effect that the bishops of the East and those who are farther off would not permit this to be done, and the letter contained certain pages of that impious one, that is, of Nestorius.

(4) And when again the most magnificent Aristolaus urged these matters in a letter chiding him,[9] he wrote again to his magnificence that certain things had been decreed recently by the bishops who have convened at Antioch[10] and that Alexander the bishop was about to be sent to his magnificence with a definite formula which had been proposed.

[4] John, Bishop of Antioch.   [5] John of Antioch.
[6] Cf. Matt 26.69–75.   [7] Acacius, Bishop of Beroea.
[8] Nestorius.   [9] John of Antioch.
[10] A synod convened at Antioch by John. See letter 66.

(5) Therefore, my most holy lord, Cyril, learning these things, was indeed very saddened at your holiness[11] because you have not "laid down your life for him"[12] who always labors (for your)[13] holiness and because, besides, you, with lord Philip and lord Claudianus, have not taken care as to how the most famous man, Aristolaus, would depart from here,[14] but acting against their advice you have done nothing. And again he fell into the recurring [illness].

(6) Now, therefore, my most holy lord, direct all your zeal to this cause. For a letter has been written by my lord, your brother, both to the most reverend servant of God, the lady Pulcheria,[15] to Paul the prefect, to Romanus the chamberlain, to lady Marcella the chambermaid, and to lady Droseria, and worthy blessings[16] have been dispatched to them. And to him who is against the church, to Chryseros, the prefect, the most magnificent Aristolaus has been prepared to write about some things which your messenger ought to obtain; and to him himself worthy blessings indeed have been sent. Moreover, my lord, your most holy brother,[17] also wrote to lord Scholasticius and to the most magnificent Artaba, so that they should meet with and persuade Chryseros to desist at length from his assault on the church; and to them truly worthy blessings have been dispatched.

(7) Hasten, therefore, you also, most holy one, to beg the servant of God, lady Pulcheria Augusta[18] so that she pay heed to Christ our Lord, for I think that now there is not sufficient care of your most holy brother Cyril, and so that you ask all who are in the palace and (furnish)[19] whatever is lacking to their avarice, although there are not lacking different blessings for them also, so that they write to John[20] chidingly in

[11] Maximian, Bishop of Constantinople.
[12] Cf. Jn 10. 15–18, 13.37, 38, and 15.13.
[13] Schwartz emended a lacuna with *pro tua*.
[14] Alexandria.
[15] The elder sister of the emperor Theodosius II.
[16] That is, bribes.   [17] Cyril.
[18] Pulcheria received the title Augusta when she became regent in 414.
[19] Schwartz emended a lacuna with *praestes*.
[20] John of Antioch.

order that not even the memory of that impious one[21] may exist, and indeed let a letter be written to the most magnificent Aristolaus so that he may swiftly urge him on. And ask lady Olympias that she also should help us and that she also ask Marcella and Droseria, because they heed her patiently enough. For there is eagerness in some [bishops] of the East to receive Nestorius. And if care for yourself would not occupy you night and day, you have many holy men to disturb.

(8) And ask my lord, the most holy abbot Dalmatius that he also should correct the emperor[22] binding him by a terrible oath and he should bind all the chamberlains lest a memory of that man[23] should any longer exist, and ask holy Eutyches that he should fight for us and for my lord, your most holy brother.[24] Let your holiness consider our most reverend clerics (who are there)[25] inseparable and let your holiness (pay heed to their counsels)[26] about this, for here some are saddened because you are acting against the promises which your messenger made to Eulogius, the priest from Alexandria. The attached catalogue shows to whom the blessings[27] have been dispatched from here, so that you yourself may know how much the Church of Alexandria labors for your holiness, since it provides so much for those who are there.

(9) The clerics who are here are saddened, because the Church of Alexandria has been stripped as a result of this disturbance. And there is due, besides those things which have been dispatched from here, one thousand and five hundred pounds of gold to count Ammonius, and now again there is in writing that he should keep his pledge. But from your church provide for the avarice of those whom you have known, lest the Church of Alexandria be saddened because your holiness acts against your promises. As you have known him, speak to count Ammonius and may your holiness persuade him of

[21] Nestorius.   [22] Theodosius II.
[23] Nestorius.   [24] Cyril.
[25] Schwartz emended a lacuna with -ssimos qui illic.
[26] Schwartz emended a lacuna with consiliis eorum intendat.
[27] Bribes. This reference to the Catalogue of bribes shows that this letter should be inserted in the collection immediately before Letter 96.

what you know and make him write hither, lest there be sorrow about this also. The most magnificent Aristolaus, who labors for your holiness, is thoroughly saddened, because you wrote such things to him. Let your holiness, therefore, ask his lady wife that she should write to him asking him to labor to perfection, and that the most reverend Eutyches should write to him. Moreover, let your holiness hasten to ask the lady Pulcheria that she let the lord Lausus enter and be made prefect, so that the power of Chryseros may be destroyed, and thus our teaching may be strengthened. Otherwise we are about to be always afflicted.

APPENDIX 5
(Alternate Version of Letter 85)

The Letter of St. Cyril on the fifth Kalends of December begins:[1]

To the honorable lords, holy brethren, bishops, Aurelius, Valentinus, but also to all the holy assembly, the synod assembled in Carthage, Cyril [writes] greeting your charity in the Lord.

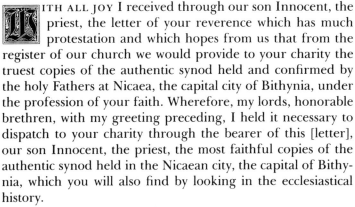ITH ALL JOY I received through our son Innocent, the priest, the letter of your reverence which has much protestation and which hopes from us that from the register of our church we would provide to your charity the truest copies of the authentic synod held and confirmed by the holy Fathers at Nicaea, the capital city of Bithynia, under the profession of your faith. Wherefore, my lords, honorable brethren, with my greeting preceding, I held it necessary to dispatch to your charity through the bearer of this [letter], our son Innocent, the priest, the most faithful copies of the authentic synod held in the Nicaean city, the capital of Bithynia, which you will also find by looking in the ecclesiastical history.

(2) Concerning the Pasch, moreover, as you wrote, we announce to you that we celebrate it on the ninth Kalends of May[2] in the coming tenth indiction.[3]

[And, in another handwriting:]

(3) May our God and Lord protect your holy assembly, that is, your church,[4] which we desire, most dear brethren.

---

[1] For the Latin text of this letter see Krusch, *Chronologie*, 344–345. In the manuscripts it is placed before the text of Letter 86 which is spurious. The date in the introductory sentence is November 28.

[2] April 24.

[3] Krusch noted that *Xma*, "tenth" was inserted into the text.

[4] Krusch noted that *ecclesia, id est* was inserted into the text.

INDICES

GENERAL INDEX

Numbers refer to letter and paragraph

Aaron, 55.28
Abel, 80.6, 86.9
Ablalius, servant at the imperial court, 96.13
Abraham, 55.32
Acacius, Bishop of Beroea, 57.3, 75.4, 76.10, 90.2, 92.1, 93.4, App. 2.1, 3.4, 3.8; Bishop of Melitene, 68.1, 69.1
Adam, 86.9
Adamantius, priest and archimandrite, 64.2
Aedesius, a deacon from Constantinople, 75.3
Aelia Capitolina (Jerusalem), 70.1
Alexander, Bishop of Alexandria, 66.5; Bishop of Antioch, 75.3, 76.9, 76.10; a priest, 55.1
Alexandria, 54.5, 60.1, 68.2, 70.2, 74.7, 79.1, 90.2, 92.8, 93.5, 106.1, 107.1, 108.1, 108.5
Ammonius, a count, App. 4.9
Amphilochius, Bishop of Iconium, 66.5, 82.1
Anastasius, a priest, 55.1
Antioch, 66.1, 68.1, 70.1, 75.5, 77.4
apple of discord, 84.5
Apollinaris, Bishop of Laodicea, 100.3, App. 3.6
Arcadia, district south of Memphis, Egypt, 76.6
Arians, 66.4, 81.1, 81.2
Aristolaus, secretary and tribune, 59.1, 60.1, 64.2, 66.2, 93.1, 96.4, App. 2.1, 4.1, 4.3, 4.4, 4.5, 4.7, 4.9
Arius, 75.5, 100.3
Arsacius, a bishop, 76.8

Artaba, member of imperial court, 96.11, App. 4.5
Athanasius, Bishop of Alexandria, 66.5, 67.7, 68.2, 69.2, 71.2, App. 2.1, 3.4; an eastern bishop, 77.2, 77.4
Atticus, Bishop of Constantinople, 75.1, 76.1
Aurelius, Bishop of Carthage, 85.1, App. 5.1

Babylon, 76.9
baptism, 55.35
Basil the Great, Bishop of Caesarea, 66.5, 67.7, 68.2, 69.2, 71.2
Beelzebub, 74.6
Beronicianus, Bishop of Tyre, 59.1, 59.4
Bithynia, App. 5.1
bribery, 94.1, 96.10, App. 4.1

Cain, 80.2, 80.3, 80.4, 80.5, 80.6, 80.7, 80.10, 80.11, 80.12, 86.9
Calosyrius, Bishop of Arsinoe, 83.1
Carthage, 85.1
Casius, a deacon, 54.7
Catholic Church, 97.4, App. 4.2
Celestine, Pope, 92.4
Christians, 76.11, 81.2, 108.2
Chryseros, a prefect at the imperial court, 96.5, 96.7, 96.10, App. 4.5, 4.9
Cilicia, 104.1
Claudianus, member of imperial court, 96.4, 96.10, 96.14; a priest, 94.1
co-essentiation, 54.6
commemoration of dead, 75.5

commingling of natures, 101.3
conjunction of natures, 55.31,
    55.38, 55.41
Constantinople, 66.3, 72.2, 77.2,
    90.2, 90.6, 105.1, 107.2, 109.1,
    110.1, App. 1.3; monks at, 99.1
Creed, Nicene, 55.9, 92.11, App.
    3.4

Dalmatius, an abbot, 105.1, App.
    4.8
Daniel, the prophet, 55.30, 55.31
Daniel, a priest, 63.1, 68.2
David, psalmist, 51.5, 52.7, 75.5,
    76.10; seed of, 55.24, 55.29,
    55.35, 55.41, 60.4, 67.3
Diodore, Bishop of Tarsus, 67.7,
    69.4, 71.1, 71.2
diptychs, 75.4, 76.1, 77.3
Domninus, chamberlain at court,
    96.9
Domnus, Bishop of Antioch, 77.1,
    78.1
Dorotheus, Bishop of Mar-
    cianopolis, 54.2, 90.3
Droseria, chambermaid at court,
    96.4, App. 4.5, 4.7
duality of sons, 66.11

Egypt, 60.1, 76.6, 86.3
Emmanuel, 55.28, 55.30
Ephesus, 92.5, 92.7, 95.1, 95.3,
    95.4, 106.1, 107.1, 107.4, 107.5,
    108.1, 108.6; Council of, 60.7,
    71.2, 72.1, 72.3, 91.5, 92.8, 92.10,
    94.5, 95.1, 95.2, 95.3, 95.6, 100.4,
    107.1, 107.2, 108.4, 109.2
Epictetus, Bishop of Corinth, App.
    2.1
Epiphanius, an archdeacon, App.
    4.1
Eucharist, 55.39, 73.3, 75.5, 83.6,
    101.8
Euchites, 82.1, 82.2
Eudoxius, Bishop of Constanti-
    nople, 75.5, 76.11
Eulogius, priest from Alexandria,
    App. 4.8
Eunomians, 66.4, 81.1
Euoptius, a bishop, 84.1

Eusebius, a priest, 54.1
Eustathius, Bishop of Antioch, 66.5;
    member of imperial court, 96.13
Eutherius, Bishop of Tyana, 54.2,
    90.3
Eutyches, archimandrite at imperial
    court, App. 4.8
Evagrius, Bishop of Antioch, 75.5

filiation, 55.24, 55.38, 55.41
Firmus, Bishop of Caesarea, 57.3,
    68.1
Flavian, Bishop of Antioch, 66.5
Florentinus, assessor of Heleniana
    at court, 96.7
forgery, 54.1, 85.1, 92.10, 100.4
fusion of essences, 54.6, 97.4, 100.3

Gennadius, priest and archi-
    mandrite, 56.1
Glaphyra, a work of Cyril, 101.1
Gregory of Nazianzus, 66.5, 67.7,
    68.2, 69.2, 71.2
Gregory, Bishop of Nyssa, 66.5,
    67.7, 68.2

Heleniana, wife of prefect at court,
    96.7
Helladius, Bishop of Tarsus, 54.2,
    54.5, 90.3
Himerius, Bishop of Nicomedia,
    54.2, 90.3
Holy Spirit, 55.4, 55.6, 55.35, 55.40,
    55.42, 55.43, 92.11
Homer, Iliad, 72.5
Hypatia, 88.1

immutability of God, 53.2
impassability, 55.33, 60.6, 64.3, 67.4
Incarnate word, 55.31, 55.43
Incarnation, 52.5, 55.18, 55.22,
    55.28, 55.33, 55.39, 59.2, 60.4,
    69.4, 70.1, 74.7; alteration at,
    55.22; blending at, 55.22, 98.1;
    change at, 55.22; confusion at,
    55.22; transition at, 55.22
India, 84.2
Innocent, a priest, 85.1, 86.10, App.
    5.1
intermingling of natures, 100.3

INDEX OF HOLY SCRIPTURE

(Books of the Old Testament)
Numbers refer to letter and paragraph.

(Books of the New Testament)

1.14: 55.22
1.18: 88.1
1.29: 80.12
1.30: 55.32
3.31: 55.20
4.24: 55.40, 83.2, 83.3
6.53: 101.8
6.54: 55.38
6.64: 73.3
6.68: 76.8
8.23: 55.20
8.58: 55.32
9.35–38: 55.27
10.15–18: App. 4.5
10.30: 55.15
13.37,38: App.4.5
14.6: 55.16
14.8–10: 55.15
14.9: 55.27
14.27: App.3.2
15.2: 51.5
15.6: 51.5
15.13: App.4.5
16.28: 55.20
17.3: 55.2, 71.1
17.5: 55.31
17.12: 51.7
18.11: 76.7
20.22: 55.40

Acts
1.9: 55.30
2.38: 101.3
3.13,14: 55.30
10.38: 55.42
26.14: 64.1

Romans
1.22,23: 55.11
1.25: 55.11
6.3: 55.37
8.3: 55.30
8.29: 67.4
8.30: 55.33
8.35: 74.1, 74a.1
9.4,5: 55.32
9.5: 101.4
10.6–9: 55.36
13.7: 92.1

1 Corinthians
1.20: 87.5
2.8: 101.3
3.11: 55.5
5.2: 51.1
8.6: 97.1
9.22: 76.5
9.26: 91.3, 91a.3
10.4: 55.29
11.23–27: 87.14
11.24: 87.14
11.25: 86.5
12.28: 58.2
12.31: 67.8
13.12: 55.3
15.20: 55.34

2 Corinthians
4.4: 55.27, 55.41
5.10: 81.4
5.20: 76.9
10.15: 76.11

Galatians
4.4: 54.3, 55.18, 55.33
4.6: 55.14

Ephesians
4.5: 52.8, 55.35, 55.38, 60.4
4.8–10: 55.35
5.27: 52.6

Philippians
1.6: 58.1
2.6: 55.25, 55.27, 55.33
2.6,7: 55.20
2.7: 55.18, 55.30, 55.33, 67.5
2.8: 55.33

Colossians
1.15: 55.27
1.15–17: 55.34
1.18: 55.34

2 Thessalonians
3.11: 83.7

1 Timothy
1.7: 55.41
3.15: 74.2, 74a.2